Abraham of Erevan

History of the Wars
(1721-1738)

Armenian Studies Series
Number 3

The Armenian Studies Series aims to make Armenian historical and literary texts available in English translations in order to provide a wider access to primary texts for scholars of Armenian, Iranian, Russian, Georgian, and Turkish Studies. Original monographs and proceedings of scholarly conferences focusing on Armenian history and literature in the modern period will also be included in this series.

General Editor
George Bournoutian (Iona College, New Rochelle, New York)

Advisory Council
Stepan Astourian (University of California, Berkeley)
Houri Berberian (California State University, Long Beach)
Barlow Der Mugerdechian (California State University, Fresno)
Robert Hewsen (Rowan University, Glassboro, New Jersey)
Eliz Sanasarian (University of Southern California)
Abraham Terian (St. Nersess Seminary, New Rochelle, New York)

Abraham of Erevan

History of the Wars

(1721-1738)

(Abraham Erewants'i's, *Patmut'iwn paterazmats'n*)

Annotated Translation from the Original Eighteenth-Century
Texts with Introductory Notes
by

George A. Bournoutian

MAZDA PUBLISHERS
1999

Mazda Publishers, Inc.
Academic Publishers
P.O. Box 2603
Costa Mesa, California 92626 U.S.A.
www.mazdapub.com

Library of Congress Cataloging-in-Publication Data

Abraham, Erewants'i, fl. 1724-1734.
[Patmut'iwn paterazmats'n. English]
History of the Wars: 1721-1738/Abraham of Erevan; annonated translation with introductory notes by George A. Bournoutian=Patmut'iwn paterazmats'n / Abraham Erewants'i.
p. cm.—(Armenian Studies Series; No. 3)
Includes bibliographical references and index.

ISBN: 1-56859-085-7
(paper: alk. paper)

1. Iran—History Ṣafavid dynasty, 1501-1736. 2. Ṭahmasb II, Shah of Iran, d. 1743. 3. Nādir Shāh, Shah of Iran, 1688-1747. 4. Turkey—History—Ahmed III. 1703-1730. 5. Armenia—History—1522-1800. I. Bournoutian, George A. II. Title. III. Series.
DS293.A2713 1999
955'.03—dc21
99-20719
CIP

انتشارات مزدا

To my teacher

Richard G. Hovannisian

Signum scientis est posse docere

The siege and capture of Herāt. The battlements of the city are depicted with Nāder's troops attacking the Afghans. Nāder is on horseback.
Source: From a 1757 illustrated manuscript of *Jahāngošāy-e Nāderī by Mīrzā Moḥammad Mahdī Astarābādī*, illustration No.5, private collection.

CONTENTS

The Siege of Qandahār in 1737. Nāder, on horseback, has ordered the artillery to fire at the city walls. Persian soldiers are climbing the ladders in preparation to take the fortress from the Afghans.
Source: *Jahāngošāy-e Nāderī*, illustration No.9.

Introductory Notes

In 1721 the Afghans, witnessing the total decline of the Ṣafavid State, rebelled and marched on the Persian capital. In October of 1722, Isfahan fell to the Afghans. Shah Solṭān Ḥosein abdicated, while his son and heir, Ṭahmāsp II, fled and began to gather support for the restoration of the dynasty.

Meanwhile, Peter the Great took advantage of the instability in Persia and invaded the Caspian littoral. By the autumn of 1723 the Russians had captured the western and southern coasts of the Caspian Sea and had negotiated a treaty with Ṭahmāsp. The treaty of September 1723, signed at St. Petersburg, gave Russia the coastal regions between Darband and Baku, as well as the province of Gīlān. In exchange, Russia promised to assist Ṭahmāsp to pacify Persia and to expel the Afghans.

Although the treaty was never ratified, the Ottomans, fearful of the Russian presence in Transcaucasia, the backdoor to eastern Anatolia, violated the Perso-Turkish peace treaty, signed in 1639 at Zohāb, and invaded western Persia, eastern Armenia and eastern Georgia in 1723. War between the Russians and the Turks was averted through French mediation, resulting in a treaty, signed in June 1724. Transcaucasia was partitioned. Ironically, historic eastern Armenia and eastern Georgia, populated mainly by Christians fell into the Ottoman zone, while eastern Transcaucasia, populated mainly by Muslims, became part of the Russian sphere.

In 1726 Ṭahmāsp attracted Nāder, a great military leader and a very ambitious man, to his cause. After a number of battles, Nāder defeated the Afghans, and by the end of 1729, recaptured Isfahan. Ṭahmāsp was installed as Shah and the Ṣafavid dynasty was restored. A year later, Nāder regained the cities of Hamadān, Kermānshah, and Tabriz and expelled the Turks out of western Persia. An Afghan revolt in Ḵorāsān halted his advance into Transcaucasia and forced him to march on Herāt. Disregarding

Nāder's advice, Shah Ṭahmāsp marched against the Turks to force their withdrawal from Transcaucasia. The Ottomans routed the Persian forces in 1731, and in January 1732, the Shah concluded an agreement that left eastern Armenia, eastern Georgia, Shirvan, and Hamadān in Turkish hands.

Nāder took advantage of Ṭahmāsp's defeat and deposed him in the summer of 1732. The Shah's infant son, 'Abbās III, was declared the new ruler, and Nāder was named regent. The war with the Ottomans was resumed in 1733 when Nāder attacked Baghdad. After initial setbacks, the Persians managed to defeat the Ottomans and kill their commander, Topal Osman Pasha. The governor of Baghdad then concluded a peace treaty with Nāder.

In the meantime, the Russians, who had withdrawn from Gīlān, following the agreement signed in February 1732 in Rašt, sent Prince Golitsyn to Persia to assure Nāder that Russia was prepared to aid him expel the Turks from Transcaucasia. In 1734, Nāder marched into Shirvan, Daghestan, and laid siege to Ganǰe. Confident that the Persians would repulse the Ottomans, Russia signed the Ganǰe agreement (March 1735), evacuated its troops from the Caspian littoral, and returned to the pre-1722 boundary by the Terek River.

The Ottomans sent a large army under 'Abdullah Köprülü Pasha to attack Nāder. Continuing the blockade of Ganǰe, Nāder laid siege to Tiflis and Erevan, while preparing to meet the army of 'Abdullah Pasha. The two armies met on the field of Eghvard and, despite superiority in numbers, the Ottomans were routed and the Pasha lost his life. Turkish prisoners were sent to Ganǰe, Erevan, and Tiflis to spread the news of the defeat. By mid-July 1735, Ganǰe and Tiflis had surrendered. Erevan held out, while Nader laid siege to Kars and ravaged the territory between Kars and Erzerum. The Ottomans sued for peace and in exchange for raising the siege of Kars, surrendered Erevan in early October.

After subduing the Lesghians of Daghestan, Nāder called a national assembly in the Moḡān Steppe, where, after repeated requests from the various tribal chiefs, he accepted the crown in the spring of 1736. The Afšār dynasty thus replaced the Ṣafavids.

Following his coronation, Nader marched on Qandahār, the only territory of the former Ṣafavid Empire still in Afghan hands. By 1738 Qandahār had fallen to the great warrior and the territorial integrity of Persia was restored.

The *History of the Wars* is one of the few primary accounts on the Afghan and Ottoman invasions of Persia and Transcaucasia. The two main Persian sources are *J̌ahāngošāy-e Nāderī* and *'Ālam-ārāy-e Nāderī*, written by officials in the service of the Persian administration. There are three important Armenian primary sources dealing with the Afghan and Ottoman invasions and occupations of Persia and Transcaucasia: *The Chronicle of Petros Gilanents'*,[1] *The Chronicle of Abraham of Crete*,[2] and *History of the Wars*[3] by Abraham of Erevan. Men of varying backgrounds composed these accounts. Petros, a representative of Archbishop Minas,[4] the Prelate of the Armenians in Russia, viewed the Russians as the liberators of the Armenians from Muslim domination. His narrative, therefore, focuses on the fall of Isfahan and the Russian invasion of the Caspian littoral and northern Persia in 1722-1723.

Kat'oghikos Abraham of Crete was visiting the Holy See when the reigning Patriarch died suddenly and he was forced to become the 110th Supreme Patriarch of All Armenians. His narrative is the account of his personal relations with Nāder during the 1734-1736 period. It is an important record of the assembly on the Moğān, as

---

[1] *The Chronicle of Petros Di Sarkis Gilanentz concerning the Afghan Invasion of Persia in 1722, the Siege of Isfahan and the Repercussions in Northern Persia, Russia, and Turkey*, annotated English translation by Caro O. Minasian (Lisbon, 1959).

[2] *The Chronicle of Abraham of Crete*, annotated English translation and commentary by George A. Bournoutian (Costa Mesa, 1999).

[3] Although Abraham called it *History of the Persian King*, it is better known as *History of the Wars*, see below for more details.

[4] Minas Tigranean, known as Vardapet Minas was stationed in Astrakhan. He was a friend of Israel Ori, one of the pioneers of the Armenian emancipatory movement, see Bournoutian, *Russo-Armenian Relations: A Documentary Record, 1626-1796* (forthcoming).

well as the rights and privileges granted to the Holy See of Ējmiatsin (Etchmiadzin) by the new Persian ruler.

The third source was written neither by a member of the gentry nor by a high-ranking cleric. We know very little about the author of the *History of the Wars*. Abraham, the son of Hovhannēs, lived in Erevan, the center of the Persian defenses in eastern Armenia. Abraham's literacy demonstrates that he was not a peasant. His awkward writing style and his use of the vernacular dialect, however, indicate that he was not a member of the clergy or the gentry. His knowledge of European words, the frequent use of military terminology, and his detailed description of the numerous wars suggests that he may have been either a soldier or was proficient in a trade that was utilized by the army.[1]

The sole existing manuscript written by Abraham himself is MS no. 2717, located in the library of the Mekhitarist Armenian Catholic Monastery on the island of San Lazzaro in Venice. This eighteenth-century manuscript contains ninety folios of three different sizes and is titled *History of the Persian King* (*Patmut'iwn T'agahori Parsits'*).[2] According to Father Sahag Djemdjemian, a Mekhitarist in Venice, it must have been written after 1738 and was probably brought to San Lazzaro prior to 1750.[3]

The manuscript[4] has no chapter headings and is written in a poor hand. It has numerous spelling and grammatical errors, and contains many Persian and Turkish words prevalent in the Erevani Armenian dialect. The narrative begins with the Afghan invasion of Persia in 1721 and ends with the final defeat of the Afghans at Qandahār in 1738.

Sometime after 1750, a student of Abbot Mkhit'ar,[5] Father Matt'ēos Karakashean of Evdokia (1691-1772), found Abraham's

---

[1]See Chapters XIX and XXI.

[2]Sometimes translated as the *History of the Persian Kingdom*.

[3]See the introduction to his edition of Abraham of Erevan's history (Venice, 1977), p. 8.

[4]Hereinafter referred to as MS A. Folios 1-64 and 71-86 are 19x12.5 cm; folios 65-70 and 87-90 are 19x11.5 cm; and folios 82b-86b are blank.

[5]He was the founder of the Mekhitarist Armenian Catholic Order.

manuscript in the Mekhitarist library in Venice. Realizing its value, he decided to correct the grammatical, spelling, and stylistic errors. He managed to transform Abraham's confused and, at times, unintelligible text into a valuable primary source. However, in order to give the text a better flow, as well as to imbue it with a proper Christian spirit, Karakashean added new material and condensed certain passages.[1] Unfortunately, he also left out important data[2] (including the folios dealing with the post-1736 events), changed certain figures, and altered several place names.[3] He divided the text into twenty-one chapters and gave them descriptive headings. This version--MS no. 2681 in the Mekhitarist library in Venice--was given the more appropriate title of *History of the Wars* (*Patmut'iwn paterazmats'n*). It contains ninety-six folios of various sizes.[4]

A hand copy of Karakashean's version was brought to Soviet Armenia in 1928.[5] In 1938 the Armenian branch of the Academy of Sciences of the USSR, using the said hand copy, prepared the first published version of Abraham of Erevan's history. Its editor provided an introduction, minor notes, and a modern orthography, and the work appeared as *The History of the Wars, 1721-1736*.[6] The text was rearranged into seven chapters with different headings and contained a number of errors that probably had occurred during its transcription. A Russian translation of the 1938 edition appeared a

[1]For example, see the material on Seghbos in Chapter III (p. 22).

[2]Material considered objectionable to the Armenian clergy, such as the conversion of the Armenian Mkrtum to Islam, for example is left out altogether, see Chapter VIII.

[3]For more details, see footnotes in the text.

[4]Hereinafter referred to as MS B. Folios 1-7 are 23x17 cm., the rest are 18x12 cm. Folios 83a-87a contain a list of the toponyms, while folios 89a-94b have Karakashean's own notes on manuscript A. The last two folios are blank.

[5]That copy is at the Matenadaran Archives in Erevan, MS. no. 8069.

[6]The editor chose to add the years 1721-1736—the time period covered in MS B—to the title: Abraham Erewants'i, *Patmut'iwn paterazmats'n 1721-1736 t'.t'.* (Yerevan, 1938), viii+108 pages, edited by S. V. Ter-Avetisyan.

year later.[1] For the next four decades historians relied on both the Armenian and Russian published versions, that is, a copy of MS B, and were apparently not aware of the existence of MS A.[2] In fact, a Georgian translation of the 1938 edition appeared in 1976.[3]

In 1974, on the occasion of the 150th anniversary of the Ottoman invasion of Erevan, Father Djemdjemian published a lengthy article, in which he included the first eight chapters of both Venice manuscripts.[4] In 1977, he finally published the complete texts, that is, Abraham's original (MS A) as well as Karakashean's version (MS B).[5] He noted the grammatical and spelling errors of Abraham's text and divided it into twenty-one chapters to match the divisions of Karakashean's text. Any additions or deletions by the latter could thus be easily identified. The new edition not only provided the original order of the pagination of both manuscripts, but furnished historians of Armenia, Iran, and the Ottoman Empire with important biographical,[6] geographical,[7] and historical details,[8] which were absent from the previous editions.

Unlike other contemporary sources, which concentrate on the political and socioeconomic conditions of the region during the second quarter of the eighteenth century, Abraham's history is an uninterrupted account of the wars between the Persians and the Afghans, the Ottomans and the Afghans, and the Persians and the Ottomans. The narrative begins with the fall of the Ṣafavid dynasty and ends with the conquest of Qandahār and the restoration of Per-

---

[1] Abraam Erevantsi, *Istoriia Voin 1721-1736 g.g.* (Erevan, 1939), 93 pages, translated by S. V. Ter-Avetisyan.

[2] They include Arunova, Ashrafian, and Lockhart, see bibliography.

[3] Abraham Erevantsi, *Omebis Istoria* (Tbilisi, 1976), 100 pages, translated by L. S. Davlianidze.

[4] *Bazmavēp* (3-4, 1974), 278-305 (1-2, 1975), 107-131 and (3-4, 1975), 284-298.

[5] Abraham Erewantsi, *Patmut'iwn paterazmats'n 1721-1736 t'owi* (Venice, 1977), 182 pages.

[6] See Abraham's colophon in Chapter XVIII.

[7] For example, see Moḥammad Khan's journey from Isfahan to Istanbul described in Chapter IX.

[8] See Chapter XXII.

sian suzerainty over the territories which constituted the former Ṣafavid Empire.

Abraham's motive in writing his history was undoubtedly the sudden and violent end of the unprecedented tranquility both in his homeland and in Persia proper. The terrible suffering and devastation, which continued uninterrupted for some seventeen years, shocked Abraham. He was an eyewitness to the Ottoman invasion of eastern Armenia and their siege of Erevan, where his entire family was either killed or enslaved by the Turks.[1] It is not surprising, therefore that Abraham has a very pro-Persian attitude and a great disdain for the Afghans and the Ottomans, both of whom disrupted the peaceful and prosperous conditions that existed following the peace treaty of 1639.

Some of Abraham's data lacks the precision of the other primary sources from this period. There are errors in the identification of certain individuals, as well as in the exact dates or order in which specific events took place.[2] Abraham confesses that he gathered much of the material from oral accounts, probably from soldiers and merchants who were present at particular locations or who heard it from other sources. This notwithstanding, Abraham's account mentions a number of individuals, events and locations not recorded anywhere else. The actions of Ramażān Khan of Hamadān and Fravodun Khan; the details of the journey of the Afghan envoy to Constantinople and his reception there; and the makeup of the Ottoman and Persian armies,[3] for example, are important additions to our knowledge of the history of Persia and Transcaucasia in the first half of the eighteenth century.

The work's greatest value, however, is its information on the Armenians. Abraham's detailed account of the Ottoman invasion of eastern Armenia in Chapters II-V is the sole source on the events that occurred in the region from March through September 1724. Abraham devotes twenty percent of his narrative to these crucial six months. The first battle of Eghvard and the role of Güç

---

[1] See the last paragraph of Chapter XVIII.

[2] All discrepancies are explained in the footnotes.

[3] See Chapters I, VII-IX, XIV.

'Alī and Yalğuz Hasan in the defeat of the Persian troops are not mentioned in any other source. His description of the siege of Karbi gives us valuable information on the role of the village elders in this period.

Abraham provides a vivid physical description of Erevan, its various districts and neighborhoods, its churches and its citizens. His detailed information on the death toll during the invasion and the numbers taken captive help explain the decline in the Armenian population of Erevan, which continued until 1828. The high regard for and trust in Kat'oghikos Astuatsatur demonstrated by both the Ottomans and the Persians, underscores the fact that the Muslims viewed him as the leader of "caliph" of the Armenian people and recognized his political standing.[1]

Particularly interesting and unique is Abraham's depiction of the resistance of the outnumbered Armenian volunteers in fighting, neighborhood by neighborhood, the larger and better-equipped Ottoman army. He delineates the roles of the Armenian clergy, in the person of Vardapet Grigor, the Armenian secular leaders, and a usually overlooked community, the Armenian gypsies. Seldom, if at all, have we read before about Armenians in this period wielding guns and swords and engaging in hand-to-hand combat against the Ottoman army. Abraham's History provides evidence that the favored status of certain Armenian notables and the economic prosperity of a number of Armenian communities in Persia had altered the self-image of the Armenians. After centuries of domination, Armenian secular leaders and their followers, as well as a number of clerics, were confident enough to take up arms against Muslim armies. The events recounted here should be viewed alongside the resistance of the meliks of Karabagh as the beginnings of the Armenian emancipatory movements. Interestingly, Abraham, like his fellow-chronicler, Abraham of Crete, does not discuss the struggle of the meliks of Karabagh against the Ottoman invasion.

It is interesting to note that Armenian troops were present in both the Persian and Ottoman armies. Some had converted to Is-

---

[1]See Chapter V.

lam, while others served in separate Armenian battalions.[1] While it is true that by paying the *jizya*, non-Muslims were exempt from military service, sources indicate that Christian inhabitants of frontier regions were occasionally recruited and released from the payment of the *jizya* for the duration of their service. In addition, the narrative of Abraham of Erevan, like the *Chronicle of Abraham of Crete*, describes the ransoming of Armenian prisoners by other Armenians.[2]

Finally, *History of the Wars* is a unique source for scholars interested in the use of language in eastern Armenia region during the first half of the eighteenth century. The text not only abounds with Persian and Turkish terms, but is a valuable illustration of the Erevani Armenian dialect of the period.

The present study is the first English translation of Abraham of Erevan's history. It relies on the Venice edition. It combines the information from both manuscripts into a single narrative. Although MS B serves as the main format, terms and figures altered by Karakashean have been replaced with Abraham's original terms and figures in MS A. Passages deleted by Karakashean are also restored. All significant alterations and deletions, as well as Karakashean's additions, are indicated in the footnotes. Modern place names, dates, and other explanations appear in parentheses.[3] Since Abraham's original text has no divisions, Karakashean's chapter numbers and headings are used throughout. I have decided to retain the title used in all published editions, with a slight change to reflect the time period covered by MS A—hence *History of the Wars (1721-1738)*.

---

[1] See Chapters IX, XVII.

[2] See Chapter VIII.

[3] The Erevan, Tbilisi, and Venice editions lack detailed annotations and do not identify most of the numerous individuals, place names, and terms (which are frequently misspelled in the original manuscripts). I have attempted to fill in these lacunae as much as possible.

Armenian terms have been transliterated according to a slightly modified version of the Library of Congress system. The same system (also modified) is used for Turkish names. The transliteration for Persian, with minor deviations, follows that of the *Encyclopædia Iranica.*[1]Commonly used terms and anglicized forms are retained, however (e.g., amir, khan, melik, pasha, shah, sheikh, sultan, vizier, Azerbaijan, Daghestan, Eghvard, Erevan, Isfahan, Julfa, Karabagh, Nakhichevan, Shemakhi, Shiraz, Shirvan, Tabriz, and Tiflis).

The Armenian Church calendar, used by Abraham, is reckoned from the autumnal equinox of the year 552. It is, therefore, 551 years behind that of the West. In addition, during this period the Armenians followed the Julian calendar, which, in the eighteenth century, placed their dating system eleven days behind that of the Gregorian calendar.

I thank the following individuals and institutions for their help in gathering the necessary material for this study: The Faculty Travel and Research Committee of Iona College provided the necessary funds to examine a number of collections in California. Hrant Bardakjian obtained copies of the Armenian and Russian editions from the Central State Library of Erevan. The main library at UC Berkeley provided the Georgian edition. The Zohrab Center in New York and the UCLA Research Library provided copies of *Bazmavēp*. The staff of the Ryan Library at Iona, once again, provided their full assistance. Dr. Abraham Terian helped decipher several complicated sentences. Dr. Robert Hewsen prepared the first map after my sketches. My wife, Ani Atamian-Bournoutian, once again volunteered to read the various drafts of this study. I am, of course, responsible for any flaws that remain.

[1]The toponyms in the maps do not contain all the appropriate diacritical marks or ligatures.

History of the Wars[1]

Initiated by the Ottomans to Seize Armenian and Persian Towns Following the Campaign of Sultan Maḥmūd Afghan[2] *against the Persian King, Shah Solṭān Ḥosein*[3]

I

How Shah Ṭahmāsp,[4] *the Son of the Persian King Ḥosein, Undertook to Regain His Father's Throne Which Was Usurped by the Afghans. How the Town of Tiflis,*[5] *After Being Devastated by the Lesghian Tatars,*[6] *Fell to the Ottomans*

On 7 April in the year 1170 of the Armenian calendar (1721),[7] Maḥmūd Shah Afghan, with 12,000 troops, left Qandahār for Persia. Hearing this, the distraught Persian nobles went to Shah Ḥosein and said, "Maḥmūd Shah is marching against you." The Shah replied, "I do not believe it." The nobles then gathered an army of 29,000 men and set out to do battle. They were defeated[8] and fled to the capital. Seventeen days later, the Afghans

[1]MS A has *History of the Persian King*.

[2]Maḥmūd (d. 1725) was the elder son of Mīr-Vais, chief of the Ghalzai (Ğalījā'i) Afghans. After murdering his uncle he took over the tribe and invaded Persia in 1719 and again in 1721.

[3]Ṣafavid Shah (1696-1722).

[4]Ṣafavid Shah (1722-1732), known as Ṭahmāsp II, hereinafter Ṭahmāsp.

[5]MS B has Mtskhet'a throughout the text. This ancient city, at the junction of the Aragvi and Mtkvari Rivers, was originally the site of various pagan shrines. Mtskhet'a became a major Christian center and the seat of the Georgian Kat'oghikos, or chief patriarch. The main city of K'art'li, however, was Tiflis (Tbilisi, the current capital of the Georgian Republic). Although the Georgian rulers had private quarters in Mtskhet'a, Tiflis, and not Mtskhet'a, is the scene of the action described here.

[6]Muslim tribesmen in southern Daghestan (also "Lezgian").

[7]The Armenian Church calendar is 551 years behind the Gregorian dating system.

[8]Refers to the battle of Golnābād of 8 March 1722.

reached Farahābād near Isfahan.[1] They laid siege to Isfahan for eight months.[2] Shah Ḥosein did not attempt to fight them and Isfahan faced famine, with the price of grain reaching six *tomāns*[3] a liter. Finally the Shah sent an envoy[4] to Maḥmūd, with the message, "Come and take my throne!" The Afghan sent the envoy back stating, "Come out and submit!" Shah Ḥosein came to Maḥmūd and was put to death. The Afghans entered the city and put the nobles to the sword, among them the five sons of Shah Ḥosein. One of the sons escaped. Shah Maḥmūd Afghan ruled in Isfahan until 1178 (1729).[5]

The stunned land of the Persians was torn by sedition. Provincial governors, following the fall of that great monarchy, rose against each other in a state of panic and subjugated the people by the sword, turning the entire country into a desolate land. Our Armenian homeland, a significant part of which had been under Persian rule, experienced great calamities. It not only suffered from the clash of arms and subsequent famine brought on by the tribal chiefs, who took advantage of the problems in Persia to rise against each other, but was subjected to incursions by the neighboring state of the Ottomans,[6] as well as invasions by the Lesghian Tatars.

---

[1] MS B has Shosh throughout the text. Shosh is the Persian Šūš or the city of Susa in Elam, whose ruins are located further west of Isfahan.

[2] They also took the Armenian suburb of New Julfa and looted it, see Gilanentz, *Chronicle*, pp. 11-13.

[3] Monetary unit introduced by the Mongols in the 13th century, worth about an English pound in the early 18th century.

[4] MS A frequently uses the Turkish term *ilçi*.

[5] Both manuscripts have a number of chronological and factual errors in this chapter. Maḥmūd began his campaign against the Ṣafavids in 1721. He took Isfahan and was proclaimed Shah in 1722. He killed a number of Shah Solṭān Ḥosein's children in 1725, the year of his own death. Shah Solṭān Ḥosein himself was killed by Maḥmūd's cousin and successor, Ašraf, in 1726. Ašraf ruled in Isfahan until the end of 1729. The best source in English is L. Lockhart, *The Fall of the Ṣafavī Dynasty and the Afghan Occupation of Persia* (Cambridge, 1958).

[6] MS B has *Hagarites*. Christian sources at times refer to the Arabs, as well as all Muslims, as the children of Hagar. Hagar, who was the maid to Jewish

It suffered the most terrible subjugation and slaughter of innumerable people—men, women, young men, virgins, children, and boys.[1]

When the calamities that we have described were occurring, a son of the aforementioned Persian king, who had survived the slaughter of his brothers and who was called Ṭahmāsp, escaped to Tabriz.[2] He set about gathering forces to fight against the Afghan Sultan and to wrest from him the great city of Isfahan, the capital of his father's kingdom. He convinced the chiefs of various regions to join him and summoned his advisors. Ṭahmāsp then gathered an army from those who had joined him and soon had some 33,000 men. He prepared, equipped and armed the troops, put them under the command of a nobleman who was called Fravodun Khan,[3] and sent them against the Afghan Sultan. He himself stayed behind the fortifications of Tabriz. On its way to Hamadān, Fravodun's army gathered additional volunteers, which increased its number to 55,000 troops. It then moved swiftly towards Isfahan and camped outside the city. The Afghans took the field against the Persians. The two opposing armies clashed and the plain was littered with the bodies of the fallen. Fravodun suffered a defeat and his troops perished under the sword of the enemy. He barely escaped with some 500 soldiers and fled to his master Shah Ṭahmāsp in Tabriz. Learning this, Shah Ṭahmāsp's heart ached and he was filled with terror that the worst was yet to come; for he had no more than 500 armed men at his disposal.

---

patriarch Abraham's wife, Sarah, and bore Ishmael, considered to be the ancestor of the Arabs, *Genesis*: 16.

[1]This paragraph does not appear in MS A.

[2]MS B has *Ecbatana, which is called Tabriz today*. It confuses Ecbatana (Hamadān), the main city of the Medes, as well as one of the capitals of the Achaemenid Empire, with Tabriz, which lies on the northern fringes of historic Media. Hamadān was an important city on the trade routes between Tabriz, Transcaucasia, and Mesopotamia.

[3]Persian sources do not mention this probably European officer, but a number of Europeans soldiers had been in the service of the Ṣafavids.

Ṭahmāsp immediately dispatched speedy couriers to the Georgian prince, Wakhtang,[1] the Khan of Tiflis, ordering him to come to his aid. His decree stated, "The arrogant Afghan has rebelled against our State. He has fought against our father, has seized the city of Isfahan, has murdered our father and our brothers, has usurped the throne,[2] and has devastated our Kingdom. Hurry and appear before us so that we may save our Kingdom from destruction."[3] Wakhtang replied, "I cannot come and leave my domain unprotected, for the Ottomans are attacking us." Angered by this reply, Shah Ṭahmāsp ordered the Georgian Moḥammad Qolī Khan,[4] who was the governor of one of the Georgian provinces (Kakhet'i), to go and fetch Wakhtang by force. Wakhtang was informed of this and together with his army, as well as numerous young men from his city, gathered on a plain and awaited the arrival of Moḥammad Qolī Khan's army. Since the latter's army marched slowly, Wakhtang moved to meet them *en route*. He met the foe in a place that the locals called Snēkh-k'orpi.[5] Wakhtang attacked Moḥammad Qolī's force, defeated it, and returned to his city.

Having lost his men and weapons, Moḥammad Qolī fled from Wakhtang and sought refuge with the Lesghian Tatars. He asked their assistance, took 6,000 Lesghian warriors and marched on Wakhtang. He planned to arrive unexpectedly at night, seize the

---

[1] Wakhtang VI, ruler and regent (*vālī*) of K'art'li from 1711 to 1714. He was replaced by his brother and in 1719 was reinstated by the Persians under the Muslim name of Ḥosein Qolī Khan. He ruled until the Lesghian and Turkish invasions in 1723 and fled to Russia in 1724.

[2] MS A frequently uses the term *t'akhtn*, from the Persian *taḵt*.

[3] Abraham's chronology here is not accurate. Ṭahmāsp's brothers were killed in 1725 and his father in 1726, when Wakhtang was no longer in Georgia and his domain was under Ottoman rule.

[4] Refers to the ruler of Kakhet'i, Constantine II (1722-1732). He converted to Islam and was known by his Muslim name of Moḥammad Qolī Khan.

[5] The Turkish word is *sönük köprü* ("broken" or "washed out bridge"), The bridge, also mentioned in a 19th-century primary source (see, Bournoutian, *History of Qarabagh*, p. 33), was located on the Khram River, a tributary of the Kura River.

unguarded city gates, move with his forces swiftly into the city, and accomplish his evil deeds in one hour. He had an accomplice in this task, the Georgian Kat'oghikos,[1] who was inside the city and who secretly planned to surrender the town. The reason for this was because Moḥammad Qolī, who was an apostate, was his relative and had promised, both orally and in writing, to grant him the province of Kakhet'i following the capture of Tiflis and Wakhtang. The Kat'oghikos himself was a member of the Georgian royal house, who wished to add Kakhet'i to the other domains he already possessed in Georgia.

In the year 1172 of the Armenian calendar (1723), on the second day of the month of May, the Kat'oghikos wrote a secret letter and sent it to Moḥammad Qolī Khan. He noted the specific day that the gates of the town would be left open and unguarded. Wakhtang was not aware of this betrayal and when a certain individual warned Wakhtang of Moḥammad Qolī's advance, the Kat'oghikos attributed it to hearsay and empty gossip. Wakhtang did not suspect his treachery and trusted him. However, he kept his army in constant readiness. Moḥammad Qolī had earlier advised the Kat'oghikos to speak ill of him and thus cleverly diverted any suspicions that may have formed in Wakhtang's mind. Thus it came to pass that on the agreed day and at the specified time,[2] before sunrise, the Lesghians unexpectedly appeared before Tiflis, entered it, and overran the city. They struck those who rose against them and looted the town. They took gold, silver and many other items, but did not take prisoners, for the defenders of the [inner] citadel, who had witnessed the attack, rose against the Tatars to stop their destruction. Thus, the latter, instead of taking hostages, concentrated on booty. At the sudden breakout of the disturbance, Wakhtang did not take any action. Instead, he took his wife and children, exited

---

[1]The Supreme Patriarch of the Georgian Church of the time was Domenti Levanisidze Batonishvili (1705-1725 and 1739-1741).

[2]MS A uses the term *sêhat'in*, which is a derivation of the Arab-Persian term *sā'at* ("time").

the city unseen, and fled to Moskovastan (Moscovy).[1] The Kat'oghikos, who had betrayed the city, left with the Lesghians the moment they evacuated the town. He joined Moḥammad Qolī and together they began to assemble a large force for a renewed attack on Tiflis.

One of Wakhtang's sons, called Shahnavaz, fled across the Ottoman border and reached the city of Erzerum.[2] He sought refuge with Saru Mustafa Pasha[3] of Erzerum. For during the hasty retreat of his father, he was left behind and had to escape to Hromastan (Rum).[4] The Pasha received him and learning of all that had transpired, immediately sent a courier to the Ottoman Sultan, Ahmet,[5] in Istanbul.[6] The dispatch read, "a son of the Georgian prince has come to me and has stated thus: "My father has been attacked by the Tatars. He has abandoned his land and has sought refuge in Moscovy. Come! Take and rule over Tiflis. I give it to you." The Sultan immediately sent a decree that appointed Saru Mustafa Pasha as the commander of the forces in that region (eastern Anatolia). He ordered that he take the son of Wakhtang and seize Tiflis.

---

[1] Abraham has in mind "Moscovy," that is, Russia, and not Moscow. Although Wakhtang left Tiflis in May 1723, the city fell to the Ottomans in June. Wakhtang and Constantine (Moḥammad Qolī) forgot their rivalry and campaigned together against the Ottomans and the Lesghians. Wakhtang hoped that Peter the Great, who had invaded eastern Transcaucasia in 1722, would send reinforcements. When in July 1724 Peter came to terms with the Ottomans (see commentary), Wakhtang, his wife, Queen Rusudan, his sons, Bak'ar and Wakhusht, and some 1,200 members of the nobility and clergy crossed the Caucasus into Russia.

[2] MS B has Karin instead of Erzerum throughout the text.

[3] The Pasha of Erzerum was Ibrahim and not Saru Mustafa. Saru Mustafa Pasha was the governor of Diarbekir. Abraham probably confuses the latter with the reprobate brother of Wakhtang, Iese, who converted first to Shi'i Islam and then to Sunni Islam. He took the title of Mustafa Pasha, collaborated with the Turks, and governed Tiflis until 1727.

[4] The Muslims gave the term Rome or *Rum* to the Eastern Roman Empire (Byzantium). Following the Ottoman conquest, the Persians continued to use *Rum* to refer to the Ottoman territory in Anatolia.

[5] Sultan Ahmet III (1703-1730).

[6] MS B has Constantinople instead of Istanbul throughout the text.

Saru Mustafa Pasha, together with 12,000 men, rushed to Tiflis and captured it in December of the year 1172 of the Armenian calendar (1723).[1]

That task accomplished, Saru Mustafa Pasha ordered a careful watch over Wakhtang's son. He was kept in chains in a house in Tiflis with six soldiers guarding him. It happened that one of the guards, a Georgian by birth, was in charge of bringing food to the prince. He was the son of a certain Mangasar from Istanbul, who was a tradesman, a supplier to the Pasha's army, and was known to the *eşik-ağası*.[2] He was given that task because he was the only one of the guards who spoke Georgian. Wakhtang's son only conversed in Georgian and therefore did not comprehend the tongue of the Ottomans. The man was thus ordered by the Pasha to carry out that task and to keep the prisoner company. During the daily contact with the prince, the guard developed compassion and liking for his fellow countryman and together they planned his escape. After several days, one night, when the other guards slept, the said man managed to rescue the prince from his shackles and that house and they both escaped to Moscovy. The Pasha was informed of their flight. He sent swift horsemen to apprehend them, but they could not find them.

II[3]

The Siege of the Town of Karbi and Developments in Ējmiatsin

Having seized Tiflis on 26 December of the year 1172 of the Armenian calendar (1723), the Ottomans secured their position there. Saru Mustafa Pasha was then told that the Afghan leader, having captured the city of Isfahan, had moved on to Hamadān and was planning to attack [Transcaucasia]. Saru Mustafa Pasha sent a mes-

[1]According to most sources, Tiflis capitulated in June 1723.

[2]Lord Chamberlain. This sentence does not appear in MS B.

[3]The Erevan and Tiflis editions combine parts II-V into chapter II with the title *On How the Ottomans Conquered Erevan.*

sage to Sultan Ahmet warning him that, "The Afghan is preparing to march on Erevan and if he succeeds in taking it he would then easily attack Tiflis and take it away from us." Learning this, the Sultan appointed 'Abdullah Pasha, who was a member of the Köprülü family, as commander-in-chief and dispatched him with a 75,000-man army to Erevan.

'Abdullah Pasha took the field and reached Erzerum, where he stayed for a month, since it was winter. On 7 February he began to prepare his advance on Erevan. On 6 March 1173 (1724) his army reached the river that the locals call Arpa Çay.[1] He dispatched two of his military commanders, one of whom was called Yalğuz Hasan, a citizen of Erzerum, and the other, Güç[2] 'Alī, to cross the Arpa Çay. Each had approximately 1,800 men. When they reached a place called Eghvard,[3] the commander of Erevan, who was called Mehr 'Alī Khan,[4] was informed of their presence and marched against them with 12,000 armed men. The antagonists clashed against each other and both sides left many wounded on the field. The Ottomans overcame and slaughtered more than 11,000 Persian troops. Only 800 men were left. The Persians took flight and together with their commander sought refuge in Erevan, where they fortified themselves and did not venture out again.

Güç 'Alī and Yalğuz Hasan advanced and laid siege to the town of Karbi,[5] which was located near Erevan, with plans to plunder it and enslave its Armenian[6] population. The citizens of Karbi, seeing the enemy, were seized with terror and began to worry about their sons and daughters. The men of Karbi, therefore, fortified their settlement, their walls, and their gates[7] and planned to resist the Ottomans. Those among them who were believers prayed to God

[1] That is, the Akhuryan River, which was one of the borders (agreed upon in 1639) between Persia and the Ottoman Empire.

[2] A variation of the Turkish term *güc*, meaning "strong."

[3] A village in the Ashtarak region, the site of two major battles fought between the Persians and Ottomans.

[4] The Khan of Erevan from 1719 to 1724.

[5] A settlement in the Ashtarak region.

[6] Both manuscripts use the terms *Armenian* and *Christian* interchangeably.

[7] MS A has the term *darbasner* (a derivative of *darvāze* or *darbāz*).

to spare them and to not subject their sons and daughters to death or captivity. The elders of Karbi, among them Paron[1] Aqa Baba and Paron Step‘an, conferred amongst themselves and decided to send a man to the Khan of Erevan with the following message: “The Ottoman army has arrived and has laid siege to Karbi. If you are willing to send troops we are ready to defend our town with our lives. We shall attack the enemy and shall drive them out.” The Khan of Erevan, however, did not respond to their request and did not send any troops. The citizens of Karbi did not think of sending someone to the Ottomans to offer their submission. Instead, they hurriedly began to fortify their homes and to close the entrances and passageways into their settlement, giving the impression that they were prepared to give battle.

They remained in this guarded condition and resisted the Turks for forty days until ‘Abdullah Pasha, who was the commander-in-chief of the entire Ottoman force, arrived with his large army. The citizens of Karbi still hoped that the governor of Erevan would send troops to defend them, not realizing that he was totally helpless and needed every soldier to defend his own citadel. It was God’s will that ‘Abdullah Pasha did not immediately attack Karbi to destroy it.[2] Instead, he sent envoys with a proposal of peace stating, “You were our subjects in the past, why have you now risen against us? Why do you fight for a State that does not belong to you and put your settlement in risk of death and captivity? Return to your former citizenship and I shall not only order my troops not to harm you, but will leave a detachment of troops to protect you.” Hearing these words, Paron Aqa Baba, Paron Sargis, Paron Avak‘, Paron Mkrtum, and Paron Pōghos were filled with doubt, fear and hope. They began to confer among themselves. Paron Manuk, son of Hovhvanēs, asked, “What if after such promises the Pasha goes against his word and enslaves us, our wives, and our children?” Paron Aqa Baba, Paron Sargis, Paron Avak, Paron Mkrtum, and Paron Pōghos said, “We should surrender Karbi to

---

[1] *Paron* is an Armenian term signifying respected citizen, similar to “mister” or “monsieur.”

[2] MS A does not contain this sentence.

the Ottomans, for we lack the forces to resist such a large army and no help has arrived." They thus agreed to give the following answer: "Give us ten days' time[1] to convince all our subjects to submit."[2] The Pasha conceded to their honest request, for he had no intention of destroying the village and depopulating the land.

In the meantime, the elders of the village secretly sent a man to the governor of Erevan, Mehr 'Alī, with the following message: "Besieged by the Ottoman forces, we had to give our word to the [Turkish] commander that we would surrender Karbi in ten days, for we cannot withstand such a large army. Tell us what to do?" Mehr 'Alī did not accept this[3] and ordered that they fight bravely and not surrender. He promised to send them gunpowder and small cannons.[4] To further inspire them he added, "Your Kat'oghikos, Astuatsatur,[5] has gone to see Shah Ṭahmāsp to seek advice on this dangerous conflict which is upon us. Have patience, therefore, until we hear some news of assistance from them."

It was true that the Armenian Kat'oghikos, Astuatsatur, was summoned by Shah Ṭahmāsp and had gone to see him, but the mentioning of this supposedly reassuring fact by the Godless governor of Erevan was totally useless and senseless. This wretched man was leading them to slaughter. He was a man of a different race and an unbeliever. He did not care if our Christian people were subjected to death and captivity. For if he was of the same faith and blood and was a true guardian of his subjects, why would he lead them like sheep to slaughter? For how could one equate a village that lacked fortifications and soldiers to the large army which surrounded it, even though the village had many men who could fight as soldiers?[6]

---

[1]MS A has the term *mulhat'*, which is a derivative of the Persian word *moḥlat*.

[2]MS A has the Persian word *moṭi'*.

[3]MS A has the Persian term *qabūl*.

[4]MS A has the Persian terms *bārūt* and *ḵom-pāreh*.

[5]Astuatsatur of Hamadān (1715-1725).

[6]MS A does not contain this paragraph.

The elders of the settlement, after conferring among themselves, rightly disregarded the words of the governor of Erevan and rather than being enslaved decided to submit to the Ottomans. After the ten days had elapsed,[1] the Ottomans sent word stating, "Prepare[2] to submit and to surrender your arms." The Armenians prepared gifts of gold, silver, and precious stones for ʻAbdullah Pasha. On the appointed day they sent Paron Aqa Baba, Paron Sargis, Paron Avak, and Paron Pōghos, whom they had elected as envoys. They were admitted to the presence of the Pasha, who asked, "How many citizens are in your village?" Aqa Baba responded, "There are some 6,000 souls." The Pasha then said, "If you are truly prepared to become our subjects, remove all weapons from the homes of every person and give them to us." They agreed to fulfill that command. The Pasha sent a detachment of troops[3] with Aqa Baba. They entered the village and took the swords and guns[4] of every defender. The Pasha then ordered that Paron Aqa Baba, Paron Pōghos, and three or four other notables be given *kalʻats*[5] and be escorted back to Karbi. The Pasha ordered six companies of troops to safeguard the village, while he himself marched on Erevan.

III
The Siege of Erevan and the Resistance of Its Populace. How the Armenians Bravely Fought Outside the Citadel and Routed the Ottomans

ʻAbdullah Pasha moved from the plain of Eghvard and three days later reached Erevan. His army camped at a site called Sambēki Dalma, which was half an hour's distance from Erevan, and was

---

[1] MS A frequently uses the term *tʻamamvetsʻav*, a Perso-Armenian compound word in the Erevani dialect.

[2] MS A frequently uses the Arabic-Persian term *ḥāżer*.

[3] MS A frequently uses the Turkish term *bairaq*, which can be translated as a company of troops under the banner of a *bey* or bek.

[4] MS A frequently makes use of the Persian term *tefang*.

[5] A robe of honor made of expensive material.

named after a water canal (Dalman) located in the vicinity. All those who lived in the villages and farms around Erevan fled and took refuge in the city.

After seven days of positioning his troops around Erevan, the Pasha decided to march on Ējmiatsin. A decree,[1] however, arrived from the Ottoman Sultan in which he ordered the Pasha not to attack Ējmiatsin. Instead, he ordered the Pasha to place some of his troops to guard it and not to allow anyone to damage it. No one was to loot it or to harm anyone residing in Ējmiatsin. The Kat'oghikos of the Armenians, Astuatsatur, was not in Ējmiatsin at that time,[2] for he had gone to see Shah Ṭahmāsp in Tabriz.

This occurred as a result of God's grace. For when the Ottoman army invaded Armenia, a pious Armenian notable called Seghbos, a most distinguished Armenian in Constantinople, who was an influential man and who held the rank of purveyor in the Sultan's court, interceded on behalf of Ējmiatsin. The Sultan cared for the Armenian people and, in the interest of the State, gave the order to the Pasha to protect Holy Ējmiatsin and to forbid his soldiers to invade that holy place. The Pasha, following the Sultan's decree, forbade his troops to attack Ējmiatsin and appointed a detachment of soldiers to guard it.[3]

When 'Abdullah Pasha marched forward with the intention of taking the fortress of Erevan, he sent delegates beforehand to discuss conditions for the peaceful surrender of the fortress. The governor of Erevan, who was called Mehr 'Alī, replied, "We shall submit your offer to our Shah and if he approves we shall surrender the fortress to you. If not, we cannot give it up on our own." When the Pasha realized that the city would not surrender he prepared for war.

The Pasha brought his army forth and prepared the siege of Erevan. The next day he approached the fortress. He placed twelve cannons in the direction of the All Savior monastery, twenty-nine

---

[1]MS A has the Arab-Persian term *farmān*.

[2]MS A has the Armeno-Persian compound word, *ēn t'arighin* (from *tārīk*, or "on that date").

[3]MS A does not contain this paragraph.

cannons near St. Madr,[1] and seven cannons on top of the three hills [across the river], thus surrounding and bombarding Erevan from four locations.[2]

Mehr ʻAlī then ordered the Muslims[3] to join the Armenians and give battle. They fought against the Ottomans for sixty days, killed many of the assailants, and did not allow them to enter the city. When ʻAbdullah Pasha saw that his army was being slaughtered, he sent envoys to Bayazid and the Kurds[4] to ask assistance. Thirty-five thousand armed men arrived, but even with their help he could not conquer Erevan.

When the Pasha witnessed the firm resolve of the citizens of Erevan and his own casualties, he decided not to continue the battle. He sent a message to the Sultan stating, "Erevan has too many defenders and I cannot take it."[5] The Sultan then ordered the Pasha of Kütahya to proceed towards Erevan. The latter arrived with 10,000 armed men and camped near the city.

Three days later the two Pashas joined forces and, after conferring,[6] decided not to delay, but to move forward. At sunrise on a Thursday they prepared the army for an assault[7] on Erevan. A large river called Zangi[8] lies before the city, and when the Ottoman hordes began to cross it, the width of the river was covered with such a multitude that the water was not visible and it appeared as if the river had dried out. Although the Ottomans had crossed the

---

[1]Persian for "mother;" refers to the Monastery of the St. Anne (the Mother of Virgin Mary), see map 2.

[2]This sentence is absent from MS B.

[3]MS A has *Turks*, which in this case signifies Muslims.

[4]MS B has *Medes*.

[5]MS B has the following sentence in parentheses "(What is Your Command? Send us reinforcements or let us withdraw)." On folio 88a Karakashean explains the reason for the parentheses by stating that he wished to convey the meaning of Abraham's vernaculer, which is *Yerevanay hzorkʻn shat ay, chʻem karum aṛnel.*

[6]MS A has the Perso-Arabic term *maṣlaḥat*.

[7]MS A frequently uses the word *erish*, which is the Persian term *yūreš* or the Turkish *yürüyuş*.

[8]Present-day Hrazdan River.

river, they could not proceed much farther, for the defenders of Erevan attacked them. These were the Armenians, who fought them for half a day, for the Persians and the governor of the city had fled into the citadel and had left the Armenians to do battle in town. Two thousand Christians fell to the sword on that day. The Armenian commanders were the following: Hovhannēs Hundibekean, Pōghos K‘ijibekean, Hovhannēs Kaṛjik, and Dawit‘ Mirzējanean.[1]

There was a certain *vardapet*[2] in Erevan, called Grigor. He went to the St. Sargis Church,[3] which was located in the neighborhood called Dzoragegh. He summoned and gathered a crowd of Armenians. At the first hour of the night the citizens sought the advice of the vardapet and asked, "What are we to do? Tomorrow the Ottomons will kill all of us and will take our wives and children into captivity." In Erevan, in the district called Kond, there lived some one hundred households of Christian *Bosha*.[4] They were wealthy, brave, and had armed men. Their leaders at that time were Paron Ghazaros Baburean, Paron Klduz, Paron Dawit‘, Paron Bēyram, and Paron Petros.[5] They and their men came to *Vardapet* Grigor. The Armenians, along with the vardapet, were in tears and begged the armed men to save them, their wives and their children from those who had besieged the town and were preparing to loot it.[6] Ghazaros said the following to Grigor: "*Vardapet*! I have two hundred brave young men. They are armed and are capable of fighting with swords and guns. I shall gather them and shall fight with all my ability." Hovhannēs Hundibekean of Dzoragegh began to gather men as well. Other Armenian notables followed his lead and promised to resist with their followers. These were: Paron P‘irigul, Paron Arzumbek, Paron T‘adēwos, Paron Mghun, Paron

---

[1]MS A has *Hohann Hundi Bēkents‘, K‘ich‘i Bēkents‘ Poghos, Kaṛchik Ovanēs, Mirzayjaneants‘T‘avi.*

[2]Armenian celibate priests, who have graduated from a seminary; equal to archmandrites in the Orthodox Church.

[3]Also known as Hovhannavank‘.

[4]The Armenian gypsies were called *bosha*. Some 100 households lived in Erevan as late as the 19th century, see Bournoutian, *Khanate of Erevan*, p. 57.

[5]MS A has *Babur Oghli* and *Petik* instead of *Petros*.

[6]MS A does not have this line.

Mkrtich‘, Paron Malkhas, Paron Alexan, Paron Agham, Paron Galust, Paron Aghazade, Paron Nuri, Paron Zohrab, Paron Nikoghayos, Paron Awetis Srapionean, and Paron Ēram.[1]

The Armenians gathered that night, conferred, and prepared their defenses against the Ottomans. At daybreak God's mercy spared them, for it was Friday and the Ottomans did not attack. The Armenians gathered brave young men from the various villages around Erevan: from Parakar, Gök-Gumbed, Kanaker, Arinj, Avan, Gavan, Dzak, and Noragegh. Nine thousand armed troops, that is, all the able-bodied men from the above villages, gathered outside Erevan to do battle. Young Armenians from the district called Old Erevan came armed under the command of their chiefs, Nikoghos, Andon son of Maryam, But‘ik son of Khatun, and the priest Ter-Movses. On Saturday morning, Bosha Ghazaros, Bosha Klduz, and Bosha Dawit‘ Bedik came to Dzoragegh with 234 men. Vardapet Grigor ordered them to hold the road leading to the Forty Mills. The men from Dzoragegh, three thousand strong, armed with swords or guns, were to defend Dzak. The men from Kond were to defend the road to the Tappakhana district (see map 2). Nine hundred fifty-five men from the Juhair neighborhood, with swords and guns, under the command of Ter-Movses, guarded the Darbinots‘ road. Four thousand men from Old Erevan were under the command of three men: Pahlavan Nikoghos, who was a horseshoe maker,[2] Andon, son of Maryam, and But‘ik, son of Khatun. There were a total of 9,423 men[3] with guns and swords, who were capable of fighting. The rest, some 28,000, were not trained. They stayed to guard their homes.

All of them left their wives, children, and those men who were unfit to fight, and gathered with their commanders in a suburb of Erevan that was called Dzoragegh. They were ready to battle for their own sake and that of their wives and their children. They placed detachments in different parts of the city with instructions

---

[1]MS A uses different spelling.

[2]MS A has the term *nalband* from the Persian *na‘lband*.

[3]MS B has 9,443 men. Although both manuscripts give exact numbers, the totals listed do not add up.

to block the entrances to Erevan. They waited in readiness to give battle should the enemy manage to enter the city and, if not, to hold their positions.[1]

The Ottomans surrounded the city on four sides. Dense gardens, orchards, and numerous ancient willow trees, which had been planted a long time ago for the defenses of the town, surrounded the city. Behind the tree line flowed the big Zangi River. Because of this the Ottomans were afraid to move on Erevan, for they could not operate their guns because of the trees. They therefore set up their positions across the river and opened fire on the city. They sought a way to advance and occasionally they managed to move forward, but only in the direction of Dzoragegh, which had no gardens or trees and from where they attacked the town (see map 2).

The governor of Erevan and all the notables were in the citadel and fought using their cannons. However, when the Ottomans came near the city, the cannons of the citadel were useless, for cannons fired from a height cannot hit the enemy if he is too near, but are effective only if he is located a certain distance away.[2]The governor of Erevan, Mehr ʻAlī Khan, had taken twelve Armenian families with him into the citadel. The most important individuals were Melik Sahak, who was the son of Melik Aqamal, and his brother Aqa-Veli, Paron Karapet, Mikayēl Barkhudarean, Babajan Motsakean, and other notables. The lesser nobles remained outside and prepared to fight. Harutʻiwn, the son of Yesaman, was sent as envoy to the Pasha. When Harutʻiwn, the Armenian, crossed the Zangi the Ottoman janissaries killed him.

The Armenians then prepared for renewed attacks. Meanwhile, 3,000 Egyptian[3]troops came to the aid of the Ottomans. They pitched camp near the villages defended by the Armenians. Being more courageous than the Turks, the Egyptians, ignoring discipline and without the permission of the commander-in-chief, ʻAbdullah Pasha, attacked like wild beasts with the intention of breaking into Erevan from Dzoragegh. Many Turks followed their lead and

[1]MS A does not contain this paragraph.
[2]MS A does not have these two sentences.
[3]MS A has *Mesra-ghul*, which translates as Egyptian slaves or *mamluks*.

moved *en masse* without formation. They thought that they alone would be able to achieve victory, gain glory, and at the same time be among the first to take booty and to accomplish their evil deeds. When the attack on the Dzoragegh district commenced, the defenders could not hold and retreated to the Forty Mills[1]district. News of this reached the Armenian gypsies, who were guarding other districts. They were afraid to move, but Vardapet Grigor shed tears and begged them to aid the defenders. Finally, 234 Armenian gypsy[2]warriors rushed to defend the road leading to the Forty Mills. They attacked with swords and guns and with God's help managed to defeat the enemy and kill 6,000. The rest fled across the Zangi, for the Christians held the high ground and the enemy the low ground. The Christians, however, also lost some 1,300 men that day. Witnessing the disorganized behavior of the Egyptians, 'Abdullah Pasha was extremely incensed and ordered that no one attack without his express order.

IV
The Weakening of the Armenian Defenders. Sending Envoys for Peace to the Ottomans. The Capture of Erevan and the Slaughter and Enslavement of its Armenian Defendants

The Sultan then ordered Saru Mustafa Pasha and Rajab Pasha[3]to march on Erevan and to join 'Abdullah Pasha. The latter received news that Saru Mustafa and Rajab Pasha would soon arrive. Prior to their arrival, however, 'Abdullah Pasha made another assault by deploying his janissaries against the district known as Kond. The Armenian units were immediately sent to that location. The Armenian gypsies gave battle, defeated them, and forced the enemy to flee. Four hundred Armenians and forty Armenian gypsies were

---

[1]MS B has Aghoreats' (*Aghorik* means mill in Armenian).

[2]MS B has 300 gypsies.

[3]Rajab Pasha was the military commander of Tiflis. He served as the governor of Erevan from 1725 to 1727.

wounded in this engagement. They did not die, but were confined to bed. After that the Ottoman army did not advance forward until the arrival of the two pashas, who came fifteen days later with an army totaling 38,000 men. After conferring with the new commanders, ‘Abdullah Pasha gave orders to attack from four directions, to continue fighting without interruption, and not to retreat.

When the Christians saw that two Pashas had arrived and had substantially increased the Ottoman army, they realized that they were surrounded from all sides and the enemy would swallow them like the sea. They were filled with horror. It became clear that no matter how many of the enemy they killed, new soldiers would appear and take their place. The Christians, however, could not follow suit, for they were locked in the city and were blocked from all sides, like fish in nets. They could not expect any aid from anywhere.[1] The Armenians gathered around *Vardapet* Grigor and said, "What can we do? The enemy is increasing its strength daily, while we decrease in numbers day after day." The *Vardapet* replied, "We shall send them envoys to discuss terms of submission and ask for peace." They asked, "Whom shall we send?" Everyone was afraid to take on this mission. Prior to this, an envoy by the name of Harut‘iwn had not been able to reach the Pasha--the janissaries had seized and killed him because they wanted to take and loot the town and did not wish a peaceful end to the conflict.[2]

An Armenian by the name of Mirza, son of Akhijan, who was willing to sacrifice his life for his fellow citizens, came forward and said, "For the sake[3] of our Lord, Jesus Christ, I shall take it upon myself to be a messenger. If I die, I will accept death gladly, and if not, I shall go to the Pasha and shall relate whatever message you entrust to me." They provided him with gifts and he left, accompanied by his servant. He crossed the Zangi River and when he reached the Ottoman camp the janissaries seized him, took him to

---

[1]MS A does not contain the last five sentences.
[2]This sentence is absent from MS A.
[3]MS A frequently uses the Persian term *ḵāṭer*.

Khan Bāğ[1] and cut his throat. When his servant, who was called Sargis, and who was from Ējmiatsin, saw what happened to his master, he fled and when the soldiers pursued him he threw himself from a cliff into the Zangi. Thanks to God he did not faint or die, but survived, reached the defenders of Erevan, and related what had occurred to his master. He added, "Woe be to us Christian brothers, there is no hope. Our sins have been great and have made us unworthy of God's benevolence."

Then the people raised their voice and, groaning loudly and mourning the dead, began to call on God to redeem them and not to deprive the Christians of His mercy. *Vardapet* Grigor then gathered the people in the church and said Mass. Having confessed their sins, they were ready to receive communion, the life-giving body and blood of Christ. Then each man stood in readiness in his assigned place.

The next morning, on Friday, the Ottoman forces, led by five pashas and divided into four advance detachments, attacked the city from all directions. The battle continued from morning until evening. Here and there Armenian and Ottoman groups continued to kill each other until the 24th hour. There was so much bloodshed that the Zangi and the earth adjoining it turned red. The smell of blood and the corpses of the dead in the town reached even the outlying districts. The city was taken on the seventh day of the month of June, in the year 1173 of the Armenian calendar (1724). The citadel, however, remained in Persian hands. The Armenian fighters thus fell to the sword. All died or were taken captive. Many drowned in the Zangi. The Ottomans took their wives and children captive, filled their camp with them and defiled them with evil acts.

Why did this occur if God did not wish them to fall into the hands of the enemy? Why did God hand them over, they whom He had redeemed and cleansed through the blood of His Only Son and had adopted as His own? He did not give them up willingly, but because their sins and waywardness brought upon them His just

---

[1]This was a large orchard outside the citadel, see Bournoutian, *Khanate of Erevan*, p. 41. See also map 2.

retribution. For their sins and unlawful acts cried out to heaven. What were the causes of their sins? Mainly it was because the clergy and churchmen generally neglected the commands of God and other teachings of Christian doctrine, preferring to take care of only the physical aspect of life. Although the churches conducted daily Masses and services, they were performed in ignorance, without comprehending the mystery and without honoring God. I shall simply state that in their soul they lacked the Holy Christian spirit and kept their Christian faith in name only and through outward acts. They lacked the required knowledge and the inner meaning of the Holy Trinity, His words of Incarnation, His Salvation and Passion. They were not only unconcerned about acquiring it, but did not strive to at least understand or learn it. Therefore, it is not surprising that God permitted the unbelievers to defile such Christians with evil deeds and to turn them away from their faith. For those who do not know God and who do not observe the commands of Christ and are careless in learning them, even if they do not experience such hardships, are not of the true faith and should be severed from the Christian faith and viewed the same as heathens.[1]

V

On How the Governor of Erevan, Through the Mediation of Kat'oghikos Astuatsatur, Received Assurances of Safety from the Ottoman Pasha and Surrendered the Citadel

The governor of Erevan, together with the Persian and Armenian notables who had taken refuge in the citadel, and who had observed what had occurred, fell into despair and confusion, lost hope of holding out in the fortress, and sought ways to save their lives.[2] During the time when the Ottomans had besieged Erevan,

[1]The last paragraph is absent from MS A. Father Karakashean's criticism of the Armenian clergy echoes that of Abbot Mkhit'ar, whose dissatisfaction led him to become a Catholic and to establish the Mekhitarist order of priests.

[2]This sentence is absent from MS A.

Shah Ṭahmāsp, who was in Tabriz, marched to Ḵorāsān with an army of 6,000 men. For he did not plan to go to the defense of Erevan with such a small number of troops.[1] On his departure, he permitted Kat'oghikos Astuatsatur, whom, as noted, he had kept by his side, to return to Ējmiatsin.

When the Kat'oghikos arrived in Ējmiatsin, 'Abdullah Pasha learned of this and sent three hundred men to summon the Kat'oghikos to his presence. The troops went to Garni[2] and told the Kat'oghikos, "The Pasha wants you." The Kat'oghikos replied, "I am obedient to the Pasha." When the Kat'oghikos arrived, the Pasha received him with honor and ordered that he be given splendid garments. He seated the Kat'oghikos beside him and spoke with him with great courtesy. He kept the Kat'oghikos in his camp for three days and continued to honor him. After that he spoke to him about the war and said, "How are we to behave if after taking the town, those in the citadel still hold out and refuse to surrender? How can we achieve peace?" The Kat'oghikos replied, "Be patient for a little while, tomorrow I shall go and talk with them and point out the necessity of submitting and they will surrender the fort."

The next day the Kat'oghikos left the camp and approached the fortress. The governor was informed that the Kat'oghikos had arrived and was standing outside the gates. He ordered one of his subordinates, Moḥammad Qāsem Beg, not to open the gate but to inquire from the inside the reason for the Kat'oghikos' presence and what news he had of Shah Ṭahmāsp. The messenger came, stood in a place where he could be heard, and asked, "Why have you come and what news do you have of our Shah?" The Kat'oghikos answered, "There is no hope of aid from the Shah. You must think[3] and decide what is best for your own interests." When the governor heard this he was filled with grief and shed tears. He then exclaimed, "Woe unto us. Our king has deserted us." He dispatched three Armenian notables who were in the fortress

---

[1]This sentence is absent from MS A.

[2]Should be Karbi, that is, Karbi-basar, a district in the Khanate of Erevan where Ējmiatsin was located, see Bournoutian, *Khanate*, p. 36.

[3]MS A has the Persian term *fekr*.

with him, Paron Karapet, Melik Sahak, and Paron Andon, and told them, "Go and find out the implications of your Patriarch's statement." When they came, the Kat'oghikos, standing outside the gate, explained the situation once again. He told them about Shah Ṭahmāsp, and presented the peace proposal of the Pasha, stating, "He promises to let all of you go in peace if you surrender the citadel." They returned and related these words to the governor. The Kat'oghikos went back to the Pasha to relate what had taken place. He begged that the Pasha wait for several days for the defenders to make up their minds and he then left for Ējmiatsin.[1]

The governor summoned his notables, among them Moḥammad Qāsem Beg, Salākhan Beg, the stable master,[2] Sheikh 'Alī Beg Reḥānlu, the chief herald,[3] 'Abbās 'Alī Beg Bayāt, Hājjī Eliās, 'Abbās Khan Beg, Ğazar Ramażān Beg, and Naqd 'Alī Beg of the Demir Bulağ district and asked their opinion. One of them, who was called Mejlum Beg, said, "I think that we should surrender the citadel in exchange for our lives. If we resist we will lose the fortress and our lives in a few days' time." The *ǰārči başi* said the following: "If you surrender the fortress to the Ottomans, then know for certain that our homes will be looted and our families will be taken into captivity, for although they now promise us freedom, after we give up the fortress they shall go back on their word. Moḥammad Qāsem Beg said, "I also have an opinion." The Khan ordered, "Speak your mind." Moḥammad Qāsem replied, "May the Khan prosper.[4] Let us ask the messenger of peace, the Armenian Kat'oghikos, to come again so that we can assess the situation." Mehr 'Alī accepted his advice and summoned the Armenian chiefs, Melik Sahak and Melik Karapet, and said, "This is what my advisors and I think. What is your opinion?" They responded, "Your will be done." Mehr 'Alī said, "We shall send someone to bring the Kat'oghikos here."

---

[1]This sentence is absent from MS A.

[2]Text has the Persian term *mīrāḵor*.

[3]Text has the Perso-Turkish term *ǰārči başi*.

[4]The Armenian word is *voghj* (to be alive and healthy); the Persian term is *salāmat* (secure from danger, good heath). The Armenian term is used here.

But they decided not to send a Persian, for they were certain that the Ottomans, upon seeing a Persian, would immediately cut his throat. They therefore decided to dispatch an Armenian to bear an official communication to the Pasha, requesting that the Armenian Kat'oghikos come once more to the fortress so that the terms of peace could be negotiated through his office. Paron Andon was asked to act as the envoy. They lowered him down from the wall by a rope, for they did not wish to open the gates of the citadel, even though they had already hoisted a white flag of peace on the citadel tower. When Andon approached the Ottoman camp, a number of soldiers surrounded him and took him to the Pasha, who asked him, "Where are you from and why were you sent?" Andon answered, "I was sent from the fortress with a letter for Your Excellency." He then took out the note and handed it to the Pasha. After reading it the Pasha immediately sent one of his officers with fifty men to Ējmiatsin to bring the Kat'oghikos to him. The officer came to the Holy See and said, "The Pasha wants you." The Kat'oghikos replied, "I obey." When the Kat'oghikos arrived he saw Paron Andon standing next to the Pasha. The Pasha asked the Kat'oghikos to sit down and said, "Mehr 'Alī Khan has asked for you. Go and find out what he has to say." The Kat'oghikos replied, "Your wish is my command." The Kat'oghikos then went to the fortress for the second time. They let him into the fort and took him to the audience room of the governor. All the Persian and Armenian notables had gathered there and waited impatiently to hear what he had to say so that they could follow his advice and save their lives. The Kat'oghikos spent a long time in discussion. After going back and forth carrying messages between the governor and the Pasha, he told the latter that Mehr 'Alī Khan wanted assurances that he would not be killed. He wished to leave Erevan and join the Shah. The Kat'oghikos thus persuaded the Persians to trust the word of the Pasha and to surrender the fortress.

Having their word that they would surrender the fort, he went back to the Pasha. He delivered their message and begged the Pasha to accept the agreement and to permit them to leave freely. The Pasha agreed and presented the Kat'oghikos with a *ḵal'at*. He then ordered some 3,000 janissaries to go with the Kat'oghikos, who carried the official document of peace.

The Kat'oghikos and the janissaries approached the fortress and presented the writ. The Persians took it, examined what was in it, and opened the gates. The Kat'oghikos entered the fortress first and the 3,000 Ottoman troops followed. The first group of soldiers immediately took charge of the three hundred cannons of the fort. The Kat'oghikos sat in the square until all the Ottoman troops had entered the fort in an orderly fashion. After that the Kat'oghikos escorted the Pasha into the fortress. The Pasha came to Moḥammad Qāsem Beg's house and alighted. The Kat'oghikos went to bring the Khan of Erevan. The Khan said, "Caliph,[1] I am scared!" Astuatsatur replied, "Do not be afraid!"[2]

After that, Mehr 'Alī Khan and the Kat'oghikos, together with all the notables and military chiefs, went to the Pasha to offer their respects. Mehr 'Alī Khan was received by the Pasha, who gave him the kiss of peace. The Kat'oghikos told the Pasha that the Khan wished to leave. The Pasha permitted the Khan and 200 of his close subordinates to depart. Escorted by the Kat'oghikos, they left and after six days of travel the Kat'oghikos returned to Erevan.[3]

The Pasha hereby ordered that all the Muslims[4] had to come out of the citadel and they did. The Pasha announced that he had to send Qāsem Beg, Sheikh 'Alī Beg, and 'Abbās 'Alī Beg to Istanbul, for Sultan Ahmet had asked for them. The Pasha then took the three men, ordered that they be taken out of town, wrapped in sacks,[5] and thrown into the Zangi River. He thus killed them.[6] Mehr 'Alī and all the others were set free to go anywhere they pleased.

---

[1]The Muslims considered the Supreme Patriarch of the Armenian Church as the Caliph (*ḵalifa*) of the Armenian nation.

[2]These three sentences do not appear in MS B.

[3]These two sentences do not appear in MS B.

[4]MS A has *Turks*, the term used by Abraham when referring to Muslims. MS B has *Persians*. Abraham also uses the term *Tajik* to refer to Turks or Muslims.

[5]MS A has the term *jval* from the Persian *ǰovāl*.

[6]The reason for this action is unknown.

When all was done and the Ottoman army had settled down, the Kat'oghikos returned to Ējmiatsin.

The Ottomans took Erevan on 20[1] August 1173 (1724). The Ottoman army rested there until November.

VI[2]

On How the Ottomans Took the Persian Cities of K̲oi and Tabriz

On the 6th day of November of the year 1173 of the Armenian calendar (1724), a decree arrived from the Ottoman Sultan ordering 'Abdullah Pasha to march on Tabriz. The Pasha began to prepare the necessary provisions for his army. When all was ready he moved toward Tabriz in February 1174 (1725). On the way, he marched on the district of K̲oi. When the Turks approached from four sides, the inhabitants of the ten Armenian villages fled to the fortress, where many other Armenians had also taken shelter. During the siege, when the citizens began to experience deprivation and suffered, a number of Armenian notables suggested the surrender of the fortress. The Persians, who were incensed at this notion, contemplated annihilating the Armenians in the fortress and announced, "We shall not surrender the fortress to the Ottomans." The Armenians then became quiet. The Ottomans brought cannons and for some forty days bombarded the town, causing great devastation and death. They then attacked in force and took the town. In approximately six hours they overcame the defenders, who were Persians, and filled the town with corpses. They took the Christian population captive. After taking the fortress of K̲oi, the Ottoman Pasha rested there for twenty-eight days. He then left forty companies to guard the town and moved on to Tabriz.

---

[1]MS B has *21 August*. If one adds eleven days (for the Julian calendar), the surrender of Erevan falls in the beginning of September. Von Hammer's date of 28 September, however, is cited by most historians, see *Histoire de l'Empire Ottoman* (Persian translation, Tehran, 1988), IV, 3112.

[2]The Erevan and Tbilisi editions have combined Chapters VI-IX into Chapter III, entitled *How the Ottomans took the Persian Cities of K̲oi and Tabriz.*

On the way, a decree arrived from the Sultan ordering Hasan Pasha to go to Hamadān via Kermānshah. ‘Abdullah Pasha then moved slowly forward, conquering the province [of Azerbaijan]. He reached the large village of Mayrand (Marand), whose inhabitants claim that Noah’s mother was buried there hence, the name Mayrand. He took it and, moving on, he came upon the town of Ṣufiān, which he found deserted. Its three hundred households, having heard of the massacre and captivity of the people of Erevan, had fled to Tabriz. After three days’ rest, he marched for three days and reached the settlement called Shor-Jur,[1] not far from Tabriz. The commander of Tabriz, who was called ‘Alā’ Qolī Khan,[2] was informed of his approach. He met the Pasha with a large force, gave battle and was defeated. He lost some 10,000 men and fled with the rest behind the fortified walls of Tabriz.

The Ottoman army moved forward and laid siege to Tabriz. Using their cannons, they began to bombard the city. After sixty days of bombardment, the wooden and mud-brick structures of the city were totally destroyed. After sixty days had passed, ‘Abdullah Pasha, realizing that the defenders would not surrender, ordered his army to attack Tabriz, while continuing his cannonade. The Ottoman army rushed in like beasts and after seven days of fighting, killed some 85,000 soldiers and took Tabriz. All the citizens, including women and children, were taken captive and their possessions were looted. After that they ceased the killing and the city was pacified. ‘Abdullah Pasha then ordered a parade and inspected his troops. He found that out of his army of 185,000 men, there were only 42,000 men left. Tabriz was thus taken and the Pasha stayed in that provincial capital for three months.[3] A month after the capture of Tabriz a deadly epidemic spread among the Ottoman troops, as if the wrath of God was punishing them for the evil deeds that they had committed and continued to commit without

---

[1]The name is a compound of Persian and Armenian words: *šūr* and *jur*, which means *salty water*, signifying that the settlement must have been in the vicinity of Lake Urumiye, which is extremely salty.

[2]May refer to the commander known as ‘Alā’ al-dīn Beg of Tabriz.

[3]MS B does not have this sentence.

pity. The Ottoman army suffered a great number of casualties. Many died,[1] while many others fled secretly and scattered about.

VII

How the Afghans Marched on Tabriz via Fāliun[2]. On the Taking of Fāliun and the Goat Fort. On the Siege of Hamadān and the Failure to Take it. The Advance on Tabriz

As I have stated at the beginning of this narrative, the Afghans, after taking the great city of Isfahan, continued to rule over it. In the year 1174 (1725), they learned of the decimation of the Ottoman forces from disease, as noted in the previous section, and moved on Tabriz with a large force. They camped by a town called Fāliun, around which were some three hundred small settlements. The Persian forces came out and gave battle, which lasted for some forty days. The Afghans put the Persians to the sword and completely conquered the three hundred settlements around Fāliun. The Afghans killed all the young men and anyone who was capable of fighting, reducing the men in that district by half. Witnessing such barbarity, the outlying districts armed themselves and prepared to fight the Afghans. They gathered in a small fort, which in the tongue of the local people was called Keçi Kale, that is, the Goat Fort. The Afghans laid siege to it. Relying on their strong walls, the defenders did not surrender, but gave battle.

When the commander of the Afghans, who was called Zelāl, realized that there was no way to take the fort, since he lacked cannons, he decided to deceive the Persians. He dispatched a messenger with a decree stating that he was ready for peace. It stated, "Do not be afraid. Submit to us and we shall let you go without harming anyone. We will also protect you against anyone who may harass you." When the envoy entered the fort through the gates, the Per-

---

[1]MS B uses the Armenian word *sataketsʻan*, a word used for the death of animals, hence implying *dying like a dog*.

[2]The town of Fāliun is 2 miles from Senne on the road to Kermānshah. MSS A&B have *Falhan*.

sians took him to their commander, who was called Karagozlu Kalb ‘Alī Qāsem Aqā. The commander asked, “Why have you come here?” The messenger replied, “ I have brought a letter from our Khan.” He then handed him the note. After reading it, the commander of the fort summoned everyone and had the words in the message read aloud. They were all delighted by the false words in the message. They agreed to submit to Zelāl and together with their commander they came out of the fort. Kalb ‘Alī came before Zelāl. The latter received him with honor and delight, ordered that an appropriate *kal‘at* be presented, and sat him next to himself. For the next three days Zelāl acted with great hospitality and gave assurances, until all the population exited the fort. He then ordered his troops to kill everyone. No one escaped. Zelāl then continued his advance on Tabriz.

When Ramażān Khan,[1] the then-governor of Hamadān, heard of this, he prepared his troops. The Afghans had to pass by Hamadān before they could reach Tabriz. While the Afghans were taking Isfahan and the Turks Tabriz, Hamadān had remained loyal to the Persian Shah.[2] The Afghans now moved on Hamadān, reaching a town called Dargazīn,[3] which had 40,000 houses. The citizens of the town were from other places and were resettled there by Shah ‘Abbās a long time ago.[4] They were of the same religious sect as the Afghans.[5] They, like the Ottomans, differed from the Persians.[6] For this reason the Afghans went there, hoping that the citizens would not only submit to them, but that they would give them considerable aid. When the Afghans came near the town, the citizens met them with open arms and exclaimed, “The Afghans, unlike the

[1]MS B has Pasha, which gives the wrong impression that Hamadān was in Turkish hands.

[2]This sentence does not appear in this form in MS B.

[3]Located in the Hamadān region, north of Arak. Also known as Darreh-e Gazīn.

[4]It is interesting to note that the Armenians were obviously not the only group forcibly brought to Persia during the 1604-1605 period.

[5]They were Sunni.

[6]The Ṣafavids had established Twelver Shi‘ism as the official religion of Persia.

Persians, are of the same sect as we are." After spending several days, the Afghans sent the entire population to Isfahan. The able-bodied youth among them were recruited, armed, and joined the march on Hamadān.

VIII

How the Ottoman General Marched on Hamadān, Came Upon the Small Town of Saidav,[1] *Took It and Proceeded to Hamadān. On The Taking of Hamadān and the Destruction of its Army*

Hamadān was not taken, however. The Khan of Hamadān, Ramażān, was informed of the approach of Zelāl the Afghan with his large force. He came out to meet him in battle near the Lailās[2] settlement. Ramażān Khan was defeated, fled into the safety of Hamadān, and did not venture out. Zelāl moved forward but could not approach the walls of the city; he therefore laid siege to it. Realizing that he lacked cannons and firearms, without which he could not take Hamadān, Zelāl returned to Fāliun, remained there, and gave up the attack on Tabriz.

When 'Abdullah Pasha of Tabriz heard the news, he wrote to Sultan Ahmet stating that the Afghans had retreated from Hamadān so that they might reinforce and resume their attack on Hamadān and, after taking it, move to capture Tabriz. The Sultan then dispatched four couriers to Hasan Pasha with decrees, which stated, "I am appointing you the commander-in-chief of all the troops in the region. Gather your troops and march on Hamadān."

Upon receipt of the decrees, Hasan Pasha gathered a large army. He possessed 15,000 men--9,000 janissaries and 6,000 *cabajis*.[3]He recruited 4000 men from Zangane Kurds, 1,800 men from the J̌āh group belonging to the Ḵazal tribe, and 800 men from the

---

[1]Either Sa'idābād or Seyyedābād (Sayyidābād). Both settlements are located near Senne.

[2]Both texts have Lalin. Lailās is a village located 12 miles northwest of Nahāvand, close to Hamadān.

[3]The term means "landless peasants."

Karaçorlu Kurds. From Taren Beg of Zohāb, who had 40,000 households in black tents,[1] he took 1,600 fighters.[2] There is a Kurdish tribe called Bajilan. They are daring, ugly and bloodthirsty, with hearts of beasts. Their sheer looks bring on terror. The Pasha sent men to this tribe and took 7,000 armed warriors, who wore chain mail. There is another tribe, called the Marjani Arabs, from whom the Pasha took 8,000 brave soldiers. There is another tribe, called Abdilavand, from whom he took 14,000 men. It took twenty-eight days to gather[3] all of them.[4] His army now totaled a force of 43,400 well-armed soldiers.[5] Hasan Pasha himself was a man who brought on terror with his hellish appearance. He had no pity and all trembled before him. After several days of preparation, Hasan Pasha moved with his entire army and marched to the district, which the local people called Zohāb.[6] The Bek of Zohāb, Ahmet, received him with such great splendor that Hasan Pasha was obliged to stay there two months. Hasan Pasha then requested that Ahmet Bek select and present 2,400 men from his own troops to join Hasan's army. The latter, who from fear could not deny him anything, took two men from each household and collected some 15,000 young men on horseback, ready to fight with armor and other instruments of war. They joined the army of Hasan Pasha and his forces increased to 68,400 men.[7] Hasan Pasha then left Zohāb in the direction of Hamadān. Reaching the district of Kasri, which the

---

[1] MS A has the Turkish term *çader*, for tent.

[2] MS B does not contain these three sentences.

[3] The text has *jam* from the Arabic-Persian term *jam*' (to "collect" or "add").

[4] MS A does not contain these six sentences.

[5] The number of troops listed in either manuscript does not add up to the total of 43,400.

[6] Both texts have Zaghov. Although there is a settlement called Zaghu (Zağe) located 11 miles from Hamadān (on the road to Kermānshah), the text probably refers to Zohāb (Zuhab).

[7] Once again, there is a discrepancy in the number of troops. The total should be 58,400 (43,400+15,000) and not 68,400.

Persians call Ṭāq Gerdūn and the Ottomans call Tak Kasre,[1] he rested there several days. From there he moved on Kerend.[2] From there he went to Harunava[3] and from there to Miyantash[4] in Kermānshah. Here God infected him with a disease. He grew numb and died after seven days.

The army could not proceed. Hasan had a son called Ahmet, whom the army wished to appoint as their commander. The officers decided to seek advice and wrote to Istanbul to inform the Sultan of the death of their commander and their desire for Ahmet to assume command of the army. The Sultan immediately dispatched four respectable envoys with decrees, which stated that, "I appoint the son of Hasan Pasha, Ahmet Pasha, to succeed his father and to march on Hamadān." Ahmet Pasha, the son of Hasan Pasha, left Kermānshah with his entire army. He marched and after some time he camped in a large courtyard called Bēst'un (Behistun),[5] guarded by Sheikh 'Alī Khan. From there he went to Ṣaḥne,[6] which was an unbelievably beautiful city. From there he went to Kangavar,[7] a large town with towers, and found it deserted, for its citizens, Persians, had all fled in fear of devastation. He passed it and went to Sa'idābād, which was a small settlement. The Persian forces, although small in number, met him in this location. The battle lasted eleven days and the defenders fell to the sword.

---

[1] Ṭāq Kasrā or Aiyvān Kasrā is another name for Ctesiphon, the capital of the Sasanids and cannot possibly be the site referred to by Abraham. The text most probably refers to Qaṣr-e Šīrīn.

[2] Refers to a settlement located 56 miles from Kermānshah (also called Karind).

[3] Probably Harunābād (later called Shahābād).

[4] Probably Mīyān-Ṭāq, which is 8 miles west of Kerend. The nearby valley is referred to as Dašt (Tasht).

[5] Refers to the Behistun (Bīsotūn), a cliff near Hamadān, where a royal inscription in relief form was carved at the time of Darius the Great (ca. 520 B.C.) and where the name *Armina* (Armenia/Armenians) is recorded for the first time.

[6] The settlement is located 37 miles east of Kermānshah.

[7] A town located 44 miles from Hamadān on the road to Kermānshah. It is partly populated by the Ḵazal tribe.

The Ottomans took the town and put it to ruins. After the sacking of that fort, Ahmet Pasha moved on Hamadān.

Since the route was mountainous and difficult to cross, the Ottomans were unable to take their cannons. They had sixty cannons and a very large one, which they called in their own language, Aslan Top ("Lion Cannon"). This latter gun in particular could not be transported. They were thus forced to backtrack and choose another route. They reached a settlement called Laklar,[1]where the peasants were extremely poor. They came to the Pasha, cried, complained about their terrible fate, and begged that they be spared. The Pasha took pity on them and ordered that no one harm them. He gave the village to one of his janissary commanders, an apostate Armenian from Sebastea, with strict orders to take care of its inhabitants. The Armenian was called Mamed (Mehmet). He was originally called Mkrtum. The story of his conversion is as follows: He lived in Istanbul and was attending to his daily needs. One Sunday he went to the public bath, undressed, and entered the large pool. There were six or seven janissaries bathing there. It is not known what he said to them, but they apprehended him and took him to prison. He then voluntarily converted to Islam and became a janissary.[2]The Ottomans then reached the big town called Salhaiva,[3]whose citizens, fearing destruction, had also fled behind the walls of Hamadān. The Pasha pitched his camp there for ninety days, but the Persians of Hamadān did not venture out to do battle.

Six days later the Ottomans moved forward and reached a place which the locals called Yangīje, which is half an hour's distance from Hamadān. The commander of Hamadān, Ramażān Khan, after considerable preparation, came out and commenced battle in a place called Lailās. There were some 300,000 Persian troops in Hamadān, according to witnesses, and they fell on the Ottomans. The Turks counterattacked and put them to the sword. The Persians rushed the Ottomans three times, but could not overcome them and fled back to the city.

[1]Probably the settlement of Lār in the Kermānshah region.

[2]This episode is absent from MS B.

[3]Probably Sahlābād, located 13 miles from Hamadān.

The Ottomans then laid siege to the city from four sides. They set their cannons and began to bombard and destroy the wooden structures in town. Fifteen cannons were positioned in front of the Zulfan[1] Gate; six cannons on the Moḵtar Gate; eleven cannons on the Sīǰān Gate; eight cannons on the Ǧaydarān Gate; twelve cannons on the Heydar Gate; and eight cannons on the Tuyserkān Gate.[2] After fifty-four days of siege the Ottomans could not take Hamadān. On the fifty-fifth day, the Ottomans attacked from all sides with the aim of ending the siege and entering the town. The armed hordes thus attacked with a great cry, deafened the earth like thunder and reached the walls, planning to break into the city. There was a great congestion of troops by the walls. The soldiers inside the fortress then simultaneously fired on the attackers with every conceivable weapon at their disposal. The invaders fell in great numbers, as tree leaves during a terrible hailstorm. Realizing that they were unable to penetrate or ascend the walls of the city, the Ottomans retreated and returned to their camp. The Pasha reviewed his troops and realized that he had lost 12,000 men in that attack. He ordered that the city be subjected to cannon fire. For twenty-five days the sixty cannons poured fire on the town, but the Turks could not take it.

The Pasha then decided to dig a trench under the wall of the town, fill it with gunpowder and by exploding it, breach the wall. In his army there was a man from Erzerum, a cobbler[3] called Kara-Bibar, an Armenian by birth.[4] He was the most experienced sapper and possessed great zeal. He came to the Pasha and assured him that he could take the city. The Pasha put him in charge of twenty men and ordered that they be given all the food and other necessary items they needed. After fourteen[5] days of digging, the sappers reached the wall, prepared a suitable place and filled it with gun-

---

[1]Could be read as Julfan. Abraham later refers to it as the Jalhan or Chalhan Gate as well.

[2]This sentence is absent from MS B.

[3]Text has *babuji* (*pabuçi* in Turkish, *papūš* in Persian).

[4]MS A does not identify him as an Armenian until later.

[5]MS B has *11 days*.

powder. On the eighty-eighth day of the siege, a Friday, when all was ready, they began to bombard the city and ignited the fuse leading to the gunpowder. The powder exploded and the wall, as well as half the gate, blew into the sky. The Ottoman army immediately sprung forward and entered the Zulfan Gate. They killed everyone who opposed them. God help the defenders. Children were separated from their fathers, and fathers from their offspring. The governor of Hamadān, Ramażān Khan, fled and survived, but the town was lost. A number of detachments, led by Shahbaz ʻAlī, ʻAlī Kibrit, and ʻAlī Ḥasan Beg, who were their commanders, held their posts and fought the Ottomans. Like people who have no hope left, they fought on for seven days, but could not save the town or their lives.

The Ottomans, after slaughtering many citizens, reached the Mok̲tār quarter. The Heydar and Neʻmatollah quarters remained. Six days later they took these quarters as well. They then looted the town, taking immeasurable amounts of gold and silver. They killed many prominent merchants and especially the cow-worshipping *Moltani*,[1] who were found in the caravansaries. They took their endless amounts of money, which they found on their persons, in chests, storehouses, and under tablecloths. They were soon loaded with cash. There was so much money in the caravansaries that a good deal of it was scattered all around. No matter how much they gathered, they could not exhaust it.[2] After they had killed everyone who could oppose them, they took the rest of the population captive: women, young men, boys, and girls. The old and the infants, and others who would be a burden, were killed. Those who were looking for captives went to the church and found many Armenians who had sought to save themselves. They took those whom they liked and killed those whom they did not wish to spare. The Ottoman camp was filled with loot and captives. In the end, there were so many victims of their crimes that the Pasha or-

[1]Hindu merchants from India.

[2]Hamadān was a major trade center on the routes to Baghdad and Tabriz.

dered the removal of the corpses from the city to avoid disease. They took them out and piled them in an open space.[1]

Among the Pasha's troops there were six very rich merchants from Hamadān, who had come with the Pasha from the land of the Ottomans. They were very well known men. The first was called Mahdesi[2] Harut'iwn, the second, Mat'ēwos, the third, Mani Manaysē, the fourth, Masēh, the fifth, Vardan, and the sixth, Mlu, who was really called Petros. They went to the Pasha, bowed to him and begged that he release those captives who were Armenian by birth. They said, "We are Christians and shall ransom[3] the Armenian captives. We will take care of them, especially since the city is still not taken and the battle is continuing. Our people and we have from olden days always been servants and tributaries to your State. You have been the masters and guardians of our people and we have been proud to be your subjects and to serve you. Following your great victory, which we also celebrate, deign to release our people. For goodness' sake and so that our joy is complete in this great celebration."[4] The Pasha gave heed to their request and ordered the release of all the Armenians. There was great joy among them. Not all Armenians succeeded in gaining their freedom, however; some were released and others were not.

---

[1]This paragraph is at the end of the chapter in MS A.

[2]The term implies that he had been on a pilgrimage to Jerusalem, from the Arabic *muqaddasi* (Turkish *mukaddasi*).

[3]Text has the Persian term *k̲arǰ*, that is, to pay the expenses.

[4]The order of the last two paragraphs follow that of MS B.

IX

How the Afghans Requested the Return of Hamadān and How the Ottomans Sent Reinforcements. How the Afghans Marched on Hamadān. How the Afghans First Lost and Then Won the Battle Due to Problems within the Ottoman Army. On the Peace Treaty and the Sending of an Envoy to Constantinople

Ahmet Pasha stayed about a year in Hamadān. In the year 1176 of the Armenian calendar (1727), the Ottoman Sultan Ahmet sent Kara Mustafa Pasha to Hamadān, and Ahmet Pasha was ordered to leave Hamadān and go to Baghdad.[1] In the same year, the Afghans sent envoys to Kara Mustafa with the following message: "Hamadān belongs to us. Why have you seized it and established your illegal rule over Persian territory? Return it to us by right or else we shall march against you and take it by force." The Pasha replied that he had to inform the Sultan. The Afghans then waited for the Sultan's answer. The Pasha sent a message to the Sultan informing him of the situation. The Sultan replied, "I shall dispatch Ahmet Pasha with a large force against the Afghans." He immediately sent four notables to Ahmet Pasha stating, "I appoint you commander-in-chief against the Afghans and am sending you reinforcements led by thirty pashas." Ahmet Pasha then began to form an army before the arrival of the thirty pashas. He gathered from among the followers of a local chieftain, called Sheikh Nāser, 24,000 armed and experienced Arab fighters. Four months later, the thirty pashas arrived with their troops and increased Ahmet's army to 300,000 soldiers. They consisted of janissaries, *cabajis*, *sipahis*,[2] *tarakelu sipahis*,[3] *meri beyraghi*,[4] *sērdēgēshti*,[5] and *talghlij*.[6]

---

[1] MS B refers to Baghdad as Babylon throughout the text.
[2] Cavalry units.
[3] From the Turkish *taraka*, in this case musketeers.
[4] From the Turkish *meri-bayrak*, which translates as "capable militiamen."
[5] From the Turkish *serdengeçti*, which translates as "suicide squadrons."
[6] From the Turkish *dalkılıç*, which translates as "swordsmen."

In addition, there were some 7,000 Kurds from Diarbekir, who were paid by the Sultan's mother.[1]

After completing the preparations, Ahmet Pasha left Baghdad with his entire army and marched to meet the Afghans. After some time, he reached a village called Ğaẕarabāṭ and camped there. His army was so large that he divided it into three groups and sent them ahead via different routes. The first group he dispatched against the Karachorlu, the second against the Bajilan, and the third he took with him to Zohāb. He had so many troops that it took sixteen days for all of them to reach his headquarters in Kermanshāh. He did not take any cannons, for the sixty cannons he had possessed previously were left in Hamadān following its conquest to strengthen its defenses. Most importantly, it was imperative to hasten and to meet the Afghans. On route, he received a message from Kara Mustafa Pasha begging him to hurry and come to the aid of Hamadān, for "the Afghans will lay siege to us at any moment." After that, Ahmet Pasha increased his speed, and, passing through Ṣaḥne, Kangavar, Mušbulağ, Sunqur, Tajlik, Tarjil[2]and Sa'idābād, he reached the province of Hamadān and camped by a stream called Zafran, which was four hours from Hamadān. Kara Mustafa Pasha heard of his arrival, came out with his army and received him with great pomp. Ahmet Pasha did not enter Hamadān; rather, he camped near Lailās, in the proximity of Gorovan.[3]After three days, he sent envoys to the Afghans and notified them of his intentions. The Afghans seized the envoys and put them in chains. When the Pasha heard this, he immediately marched against the Afghans. He reached Mārān[4]but there was still no sign of the Afghan army. He moved on to Ḵazalkend[5]but the Afghans were not there. From there he proceeded to Tarija, which is in the direction

[1]MS B has *There were Turks, Medes, Assyrians, Babylonians, Arabs, and numerous people of various ethnic groups.*

[2]Probably refers to the villagė of Taǰareh, in the vicinity of Senne on the Hamadān-Tehran road.

[3]Probably Govāver, a settlement south of Kerend.

[4]Mārān lies 25 miles west of Hamadān.

[5]Probably the village of Ḵazal, located in the Hamadān region.

of Changavan. The Ottoman army was so large that soldiers did not recognize each other.

Six days after the arrival of the Ottomans, the Afghans appeared with a large army and the battle commenced. In the first encounter, the Afghans suffered defeat and took flight. In the second encounter, however, the Ottomans were beaten and ran all the way to Hamadān. Rumors began to circulate among the Ottoman troops. Some said that they saw flames pouring down on them from the sky. Others said numerous winged snakes attacked them. Others swore that during the battle the ground shifted as if it were the sea. The Ottoman army was filled with such fantasies. According to some soldiers, the cause of these troubles was the Afghan ruler, who was very knowledgeable in the art of magic, had succeeded in stunning them with all sorts of hallucinations. It is unknown for certain if the Afghan ruler used magic or not. But we have other explanations. The Afghans, unlike the Persians, are of the same religion as the Ottomans (Sunni); thus, when they fought the Turks they probably said to themselves, "They are our brothers, how can we kill them?" In addition, when the Ottomans are not fighting to capture a city, which would give them booty, as well as captive women and children, they do not commit themselves and flee at the slightest problem. There was also another reason. The father of the Afghan ruler was called *Amir* and his son had taken the name of Amir-Vais.[1] When the Turks heard the name shouted about they thought it was the genuine *amir*[2] of the Muslims, whom they regard highly and against whom they would not raise their weapons for fear of offending him. The rumor spread that he was the true *amir* and since they had risen against him, they had sinned and were thus defeated. This, I think, was probably the main reason for their retreat.

---

[1]The author is mistaken. The Afghan ruler was Maḥmūd, who was the nephew of Mir-Vais.

[2]The Turks probably confused him with *Amir ul-mu'minin* ("the commander of the faithful") a title of the caliph. MS A has *seyyed* (related to the family of the Prophet Muḥammad).

When Ahmet Pasha realized that his army had lost its nerve, he lost heart and gave up the idea of victory over the enemy. He conferred with his officers and sent a message to the Sultan in Istanbul informing him of the rumors that had spread among the troops. He added that the situation was dangerous and advised concluding peace with the Afghans. The Sultan so ordered. Ahmet Pasha then sent an envoy to the Afghan ruler with the following message: "Our Sultan wishes to conclude a peace with you." The Afghans received the envoy with great respect and dispatched their own envoy, one of their notables called Moḥammad Khan Baluč, with a large elephant[1] bearing superb gifts and jewels to the great Sultan in Istanbul.[2]

The envoy left Isfahan for Istanbul. On the way he stopped in Hamadān, where he was treated with honor by Kara Mustafa Pasha, who kept him for ten days. He then continued his journey for eighteen days, and via Zafran, Sa'idābād, Kangavar, Ṣaḥne, Behistun, Kermānshah, Miyantash, Harunābād, Kerend, Taq Kasra, and Zohāb, reached Baghdad. Ahmet Pasha entertained him there with great pomp for twenty-eight days. The envoy then went on a pilgrimage to the sacred places known as Imam Aqā and Imam 'Abbās.[3] He then left for Tabalu and Kirkuk. In Kirkuk he was greeted with honor by the local governor, 'Ali Ahandi, who feted him for eight days. He then went to Baba Gurgur, called so because if one digs a hole, fire and smoke come out from the ground. He found the place comfortable and rested there for six days. He then traveled to Gök-Täppä, Evril, and after crossing a number of settlements, reached Mosul. The envoy, as stated, had a large elephant with him as part of the gifts to the Sultan. The animal's foot got infected and it could not go on. The envoy decided to leave the

---

[1]MS A has the Persian term *fil*.

[2]Folio **33a** of MS B is a single page (33b is empty). The information presented there is very condensed. It has only the following sentence: *The envoy took the long journey to Baghdad, then Syria (Asorestan*, that is, Assyria, in this case Syria) *and finally to his destination in the land of the Greeks* (*Hunastan*, in this case Byzantium/Rum).

[3]Probably Naǰaf and Karbalā.

beast, with orders that he be sent on after recovering. He left two men in charge of the elephant. A day later a messenger caught up with the envoy and presented a letter from the Afghan ruler, which stated, "Rush to Istanbul, stay there a month and return immediately, for the Persian Shah's son, Ṭahmāsp, has gathered a force in K̲orasan and is planning to march against us."

The terrified envoy hurried to Istanbul via Diarbekir and came to Boli, which is a district located six or seven days from Istanbul. He continued on to Baraja and reached Izit, where he remained for seven days. The Sultan sent the commander-in-chief of the janissaries[1] to meet him and to escort him to Üsküdar. The envoy stayed there for two days and was then taken to Istanbul. He went through the Yeni (Yengi) Bağçe Gate, the Divan, the Yeni Ğışli, Sali Bazaar, Kara Gümrük, the Edirne Gate, and Eyyub Sultan to Čiftlak, where he stayed for three days. Here he received news that the elephant had died on the way to Istanbul in a settlement called Armutan in Diarbekir. The envoy then took the magnificent gifts that he had brought for the Sultan and was admitted to his presence. The Sultan was greatly pleased and presented the Afghans with gifts. The envoy received an expensive *kal'at*, while the entire Afghan delegation was given gifts as well as money, each according to his rank. The Afghan envoy had five hundred[2] Afghan cavalrymen and fifteen Armenian *zamburakčīs*. The *zamburaks* were small guns mounted on camels,[3] each holding one-and-a-half liters[4] of lead. Five of these Armenians were from Erevan. They were: Avak, Astuatsatur, Harut'iwn Baba, Akhijan, Dawit', and Minas. The rest were from the Armenian villages in P'eria, which is five hours distance from Isfahan.[5] The envoy was permitted to leave Istanbul after sixty days. He returned via Üsküdar and after

[1]Text has the Turkish term *yeniçeri ağası.*

[2]MS B has *100.*

[3]These were the swivel cannons known as *zamburak.*

[4]One liter equals 7.2 kg.

[5]The Armenian settlement in present-day Daran-Ak̲ora region, 95 miles west of Isfahan.

ninety-nine days reached Hamadān, where he rested for thirteen days.

While the envoy was performing his duties, many things happened to the Afghans who were in Isfahan. Their ruler, Maḥmūd,[1] who was a magician, was consumed by evil spirits, fell into a fit, tore his body with his own teeth, and died. In his place sat Shah Ašraf. Soon after, Shah Ṭahmāsp, who with the help of Qolī Khan[2] had become more powerful, regained the city of Isfahan from the Afghans. When the Afghan envoy reached Hamadān, he received a letter from Isfahan that Shah Ṭahmāsp, the son of Shah Ḥosein, had defeated the Afghan army and had recaptured Isfahan. Hearing such news, the envoy decided not to go to Isfahan and stayed in Hamadān.

The envoy stayed in Hamadān for another thirty-five days. 'Abdul Rahman Pasha, who was the governor of Hamadān at the time, inquired if the envoy planned to go to Isfahan. The envoy replied that he was afraid to go. The Pasha then said, "Wait awhile. I shall write to the Sultan for instructions." He then informed the Sultan of what had occurred in Isfahan and asked what to do with the envoy. The Sultan responded, "I have given many precious jewels to the envoy as gifts for the Afghan Shah. Take them back and let him go to Isfahan." The Pasha did as he was instructed. The envoy begged him, however, to appoint him as his (the Pasha's) envoy to Shah Ṭahmāsp. The Pasha agreed and dispatched him with 200 horsemen to Isfahan. Upon arrival the Shah asked him, "Who are you and where do you come from?" The envoy replied, "May God protect you! The Afghans had sent me to Istanbul and I have returned." The Shah said, "To whom shall you report[3] now that the Afghans have gone?" The envoy replied, "I was a great noble in your father's service; God took your father's throne and God has

---

[1]Text has Mir-Vais.

[2]Hereinafter Nāder. MS B has Qolī Khan and MS A has Tahmaz (Ṭahmāsp) Khan or Ṭahmāsp Qolī. Both refer to Nadr/Nāder Khan (later Nāder Shah) of the Afšār tribe, who joined Shah Ṭahmāsp, taking the title Ṭahmāsp Qolī Khan (Slave of Ṭahmāsp or, more appropriately, "one who serves Ṭahmāsp").

[3]Text has the Persian term *ǰavāb* (answer).

now returned it to you. I wish to serve you in my previous position." The Shah agreed and the envoy did not return to the Ottomans and did not report to the Afghans.[1] Finally, 'Abdul Rahman Pasha wrote to the Sultan and informed him that he had retrieved the gifts, and had dispatched the envoy to Isfahan, but the latter had not returned. Three months later, a Catholic Armenian from Isfahan, called Sarukhan, arrived at Father Anthony's church in Hamadān. The Pasha sent two or three lackeys[2] to fetch him. The Pasha asked, "What news do you have from Isfahan?" The Armenian replied, "Your envoy arrived and the Shah appointed him as one of his khans. He shall not return."[3]

How Shah Ṭahmāsp recaptured Isfahan we shall relate in the next chapter.

X[4]

How With Nāder's Help Shah Ṭahmāsp Regained the City of Isfahan and Ascended His Father's Throne

As we noted in the beginning of this narrative, Shah Ṭahmāsp, the son of Shah Ḥosein, took it upon himself to restore the throne of his father, which was usurped by the Afghans. However, due to the civil strife caused by the Afghans in Persia, the provincial governors had severed their contacts with the central government. They had gone on their own and the Afghans had subdued some. Shah Ṭahmāsp, who, by right of succession, was their leader, began to summon them to join him as a single unit. They did not submit and he, like a head that was severed from the limbs, could not do any-

---

[1]According to Persian contemporary sources, Nāder met Moḥammad Khan Balūč, the envoy to Constantinople (see previous chapter), in Dezfūl (and not in Isfahan). After the latter had submitted to him, Nāder appointed him the governor of Kūhgīluye, see *Jahāngošā-ye Nāderi*, p. 117.

[2]Text has the Persian term *čokedar*.

[3]This paragraph does not appear in MS B.

[4]The Erevan and Tbilisi editions have retained this chapter intact (including the heading). It appears as Chapter IV.

thing about it. After a few years of effort in this direction, with the help of Almighty God, who, through His judgement and will allots the due of governments as well as that of all believers and unbelievers, he managed, with the assistance of one of his notables, called Ṭahmāsp Qolī (Nāder), to achieve his goal. Nāder was a lucky man in this transient life. He was also a man of common sense in worldly affairs and a great warrior from his youth.[1]

In the year 1177 of the Armenian calendar (1728), Shah Ṭahmāsp, who had heard of the military ability of Nāder, sent envoys inviting him to his camp and appointed him commander of all his forces with the intention of marching on Isfahan. Nāder replied, "I accept your order with pleasure, but I have one request. If you fulfill it I shall accomplish the task, otherwise I will not. You must grant me full power to govern the land. You will stand above me. You will stay on your throne and will not interfere in any military decisions, leaving them solely to me." Shah Ṭahmāsp agreed. He trusted Nāder's loyalty and granted him his wish. Nāder then inspected the thousands of armed men under his command and prepared to march against the Afghans with the intention of subduing or killing everyone who did not submit to the Persian king.[2]

He marched against every city and every province and conquered them. He reached the city of Isfahan and camped on the plain near the city. Ašraf, the ruler of the Afghans, heard this and moved against him with a large force. They fought for many days and filled the plain with corpses. The Afghans were defeated and fled into the city. Nāder followed them and laid siege to the city. Several days later, while Nāder awaited a second battle, the Afghans secretly left Isfahan from the gates located on the other side of the city and fled with a huge booty gathered from the citizens. Nāder, who did not suspect this and who was preparing for war, soon realized that the enemy was not showing himself. The Persians smashed the gates, rushed into the city and, finding it empty [of troops], realized what the Afghans had done. This is how Isfa-

[1]This paragraph does not appear in MS A.
[2]This paragraph does not appear in MS A.

han was taken. Shah Ṭahmāsp then entered and ascended the throne of his father.[1]

After taking Isfahan, Nāder marched toward Shiraz. The Afghan ruler had fled, had reached the city of Shiraz, and had joined two of his chiefs, called J̌elāl and Molla Za'farān Khan. They had some 6,000-7000 troops. Za'farān Khan and his forces were stationed a three-days' march from Shiraz and had camped by the river called Ab-e Kuran,[2] which flows down from the Baḵtiyārī region near Shiraz. Nāder attacked and routed the army of Za'farān Khan. Za'farān Khan barely escaped and fled. Crossing a bridge, the soldiers of Nāder overtook him and he jumped in the river, swam across it and saved himself. Nāder and his army marched on to Shiraz. He did not attack the city but pitched his camp on an open plain. The Afghans came out and gave battle. It was a terrible conflict. The Afghans lost and fled.

Shah Ṭahmāsp ascended the throne of his father and sent envoys to the Ottoman Sultan with letters which stated, "Return my cities, which you seized during the Afghan occupation. For now, with the help of God, I have defeated the Afghans and have expelled them from my county. I have taken Isfahan and my father's throne has passed on to me." He also sent envoys with letters to the Tsar of Moscovy[3] for the return of Gīlān. The Ottoman Sultan did not rush to answer Shah Ṭahmāsp, for he did not want to freely surrender the towns, which he had taken by force. Moscovy, however, answered thus: "In order to protect your cities from devastation, I, at great expense, took Gīlān and have protected it ever since. If you return all the expenses which we have incurred, as well as the interest, which amounts to 80,000 tomāns a year, I shall return it to you." Shah Ṭahmāsp agreed to pay the sum. Moscovy evacuated Gīlān, made a peace treaty[4] with Persia by which Shah

---

[1]This occurred on 7 December 1729, see *A Chronicle of the Carmelites*, I, 582. This paragraph does not appear in MS A.

[2]The Kor River.

[3]Tsar Peter II (1727-1730).

[4]The treaty in question was signed in Rašt (1732).

Ṭahmāsp was to pay 80,000 tomāns a year, and returned to its land.[1]

Nāder concluded his campaign in Shiraz and moved on Yazd. There were many Afghans there. There was also an Ottoman Pasha called Timur. The moment he heard that Nāder was on the move, he decided to flee. He gathered his well armed one hundred horsemen, who were among the Afghan army, and with the help of the Karagozlu tribe, escaped to Hamadān, which was held by the Ottomans. He did not enter Hamadān, but camped outside it in an abandoned fortress called Zahtarān, which he occupied with his cavalrymen.

Nāder marched from Shiraz and reached Yazd. He fought the Afghans and put them to the sword. Only those who fled saved their lives. Nāder stayed in Yazd for twenty-eight days. After that, he turned and went toward Isfahan. The moment Shah Ṭahmāsp heard of his approach, he dispatched couriers with the following message: "The Lor, that is, the Bak̲tīyāri forces,[2] have gathered. They are attacking our villages and taking captives. Attack them!" Nāder marched for fourteen days, reached the Bak̲tīyāris and smashed them. Upon hearing this, Shah Ṭahmāsp was ecstatic and sent a superb *kal'at* to his commander.

After this, Nāder sent a message to the Shah that he intended to march on Dezfūl and Šūštar. For the population of Dezfūl and Šūštar had risen against the Persians and had devastated twenty-six villages, taking their population captive. Shah Ṭahmāsp dispatched a letter authorizing Nāder to kill anyone who had risen against his rightful rule. Nāder reached Dezful and Šūštar and fought its people for fourteen days. He defeated them, created a river of blood, and took 15,000 households captive, which he sent to K̲orāsān, which is Mašhad.[3] When Shah Ṭahmāsp heard the news, he was overjoyed and ordered Isfahan to be decorated with silk and lights and declared a holiday for many days. The main reason for the de-

---

[1]MS A does not contain this paragraph.

[2]The Lor-Bak̲tīyāri are discussed in more detail in Chapter XVI.

[3]Mašhad is the main city of the K̲orāsān province. Both manuscripts, however, view the two as one entity or use them interchangeably.

feat of the Baḵtiyaris and the inhabitants of Dezfūl-Šūštar was that although they had been allies, they had argued with each other. Thus, when Nāder attacked them, they did not help each other and he managed to defeat them separately with only some 7,000 men.

When the constable of the Duḵtarān fort heard of Nāder's success, he began to make preparations. He gathered 145,000 men, brought them to his fort, and waited. In the meantime, the people belonging to the region of Hawuz,[1] under the leadership of 'Alī Mardān Khan,[2] also readied themselves.[3]

After these victories, Nāder sent a message to Shah Ṭahmāsp to inform him of what had occurred and added, "I now want to march against the Ottomans." Shah Ṭahmāsp did not wish it and answered, "I have sent an envoy to them to return our cities, which they occupied during our misfortunes. I have demanded some kind of an answer. I have waited for a long time and have heard nothing from them. Wait a while longer and in the meantime have your army ready to march against the Ottomans." The envoy, by the way, was 'Abdul Bašī Khan, a relative of Sheikh 'Alī Khan of Kermānshah.[4]

XI[5]

How Nāder Captured Hamadān From the Ottomans

After the Afghan Khans were expelled from Persia, Shah Ṭahmāsp dispatched ambassadors to the Ottoman court in Istanbul demanding the return of the towns that they had stolen from him. At that time the Pasha of Hamadān was a man called 'Abdul Rahman. He

---

[1] Also known as Hovizeh, is 65 miles north of Mohammareh (present-day Ḵorramšāhr).

[2] Not to be confused with 'Alī Mardān Khan Šāmlū, Nāder's envoy to India.

[3] MS B does not have this paragraph. Karakashean is accurate when he notes that he left it out because it was undecipherable and did not follow the material in the text.

[4] This sentence does not appear in MS B.

[5] The Erevan and Tbilisi editions have retained the heading, but have combined Chapters XI-XII into Chapter V.

learned that Nāder was gathering troops to march on Hamadān. He immediately sent a message to Sultan Ahmet in Istanbul, which stated, "The Persians are preparing to make war on us." The Sultan replied, "Make preparations to resist them. I shall send an army to help you." The Sultan then sent a message to the Pasha of Diarbekir[1] ordering him to gather a large army and to proceed to Hamadān, for the Persians[2] were on the move. The Pasha gathered from among the Kurds in the Mush province those who could swing a sword, and with some 33,000 men marched on Hamadān. He joined the Turkish forces already there and his army increased to 45,000 men. The Ottoman Sultan, in the meantime, received the Persian ambassador and kept him under house arrest. He did not hurry with his answer to the Shah, preparing all the time for war. The Persians became aware and prepared 12,000 men for war. The Pasha of Hamadān, 'Abdul Rahman, again wrote to the Sultan stating: "Our troops are few and are not enough to fight against the Persian forces." The Sultan wrote to the Pasha of Edessa, which is also called Urfa, to send fighters to Hamadān. He gathered 7,000 troops from among the Kurds, all of them cut-throats, appointed a man called Tokhmakh as their leader, and dispatched them to Hamadān. When they arrived, 'Abdul Rahman ordered them to go to a place called Nahāvand, three-days' distance from the Persian town of Ulugerd.

The moment that Nāder became aware that the Persian envoy was in chains, he realized that the Ottomans were not planning to surrender the cities peacefully, but were preparing for war. He, therefore, also began to reinforce and increased his army from 7,000 to 12,000 men. He then marched towards Ulugerd, which was a three-days' march from Nahāvand. The Ottoman army met him. They faced each other for twenty-nine days and neither commenced an attack. Finally, Nāder sent an envoy to 'Abdul Rahman Pasha in Hamadān stating: "Surrender Hamadān, which you took during our time of troubles, peacefully, or we shall take it by

---

[1]MS B has *Amida*.

[2]Text has *Kızılbaş*, that is, the followers of the Ṣafavids who wore red caps. The Ottomans referred to the Persians as the *Kızılbaş*.

force." 'Abdul Rahman replied, "Give us ten days to confer and we shall give an answer to your proposal." The reason for this was that 'Alī Pasha, who was the Grand Vizier of the Sultan, had sent a secret message to him, to Ibrahim, the Pasha of Tabriz, and to Husein, the Pasha of Senne,[1]stating that if and when Nāder laid seige to the city, they should give up Hamadān and not fight. The Sultan was not told of this. That is why 'Abdul Rahman requested time so that he could follow the instructions of the Grand Vizier and prepare the surrender of Hamadān. The reason 'Alī Pasha's order was kept secret was that if it were made public, his enemies would gather and would convince the Sultan to execute him. Even worse, they might have plotted to remove the Sultan from the throne.[2]

Meanwhile, Hasan, the Pasha of Kermānshah, and Timur Pasha, who as noted before had fortified the fortress of Zahtarān, were not aware of the secret order of the vizier, for the latter had not sent them a similar letter. 'Abdul Rahman Pasha asked Timur Pasha to come to Hamadān. Three days later, the latter arrived with his troops, some 6,000 men. When the two pashas met, Timur said, "Let us take all the cannons from the fortress and launch a surprise attack against the Persians with all our forces before they can lay siege to the city." 'Abdul Rahman Pasha answered, "We cannot do that, for we have no orders from the Sultan or from him who is second in command (Grand Vizier) to take the cannons out of the fort and to attack Nāder. I have instructions to remain in the fortress to defend it with my 90,000-man army,[3] while you and your 6,000 men attack him." He then sent Timur Pasha with his 6,000 men to face Nāder, who was approaching Hamadān.

Timur Pasha marched forward and reached a place near Ulugerd, where he set up camp near a stream called Āb-e Mūš, which in Persian means the Mouse Stream and which is some six-

[1]Present-day Sanandaǰ, west of Hamadān.

[2]MS A does not contain the last two sentences.

[3]MS B does not have "9000-man army." In any case the numbers do not correspond with the text (should be 45,000). The number of troops is inconsistant throughout both manuscripts.

hours' distance from Hamadān. He remained there for one day. Nāder was informed of his arrival and attacked with 12,000 of his best men. The two armies cut each other down for three hours. Timur's forces suffered defeat and, taking advantage of nightfall, fled into Hamadān. They traveled the distance of six days in twenty-four hours. Timur's troops went into Hamadān. Timur himself took refuge in his own fort, which as noted, was called Zahtarān. When 'Abdul Rahman Pasha heard the news, he immediately took his wives, sons, and daughters and, with his 45,000-man army, fled that same night. In the morning there was not a single Turk left in the city. They had all scattered. Nāder at first feared that Timur would gather forces and attack him. He therefore moved on the fort of Zahtarān, planning to lay siege to it. But Timur fled from there and went to Tabriz, which at that time was still in Ottoman hands. Nāder could not catch him. The vizier's letter to 'Abdul Rahman and the other pashas fell into Timur Pasha's hand. He kept it a secret and held it on his person. For almost two months he did not breathe a word of it to the Pasha of Tabriz. Meanwhile, after three days, Nāder entered Hamadān and found it abandoned. That is how he took that city. For many days thereafter his men caught Ottoman soldiers, brought them to him and he ordered that they be put to death. Nāder stayed in Hamadān for thirty-three days.

The Persians then found five Christians, four Armenians and one Assyrian. They had come from the land of the Ottomans. One, called Sarukhan, was from Baghdad, and another, called Hana, was from Istanbul. They were both Catholics.[1] A third, Kara Bibar, was from Erzerum and was a tunnel digger, the fourth, called T'oṛun, was from Mush, while the fifth, called Ardi, was an Assyrian from Mosul.[2] They were merchants[3] who were trapped in the city. The Catholic priest[4] had given them shelter. The Persians found them,

---

[1]This information is, ironically, absent from MS B. Sarukhan is also mentioned in Chapter IX.

[2]Kara Bibar, as noted earlier, was a sapper. The rest of them were merchants.

[3]Text has the Persian term *bazargan*.

[4]Text has the Latin *Pater*.

beat them, and planned to kill them. A Christian by the name of Manaysē stopped them and said, "They are Armenians. Take them to Nāder, who will decide their fate." They were brought to him. He asked them who they were, where they came from, and what they possessed. They brought a number of witnesses and informed him that they were merchants. They presented their wares. Nāder then asked what was the worth of each man's merchandise. Sarukhan, who was from Baghdad, replied, "I brought much silk[1] and other goods to sell to your troops. One of your soldiers has taken silk worth six purses;[2] *panzar*[3] and *yashmaz*[4] worth twenty-four purses; *keçe*[5] worth sixteen purses; furs, *lakhum*,[6] *sadraj*,[7] *jleghayva*,[8] and *ruvand*[9] worth 175 purses. He has refused to pay or to return the merchandise." Nāder asked, "Can you identify him?" Sarukhan replied, "Yes I can!" Nāder then ordered that he be found and brought before him. When he ascertained that everything that the merchant had said was the truth, he took everything away from the soldier and ordered that it be taken to his tent. He then told the Armenian merchant, "I will not kill you. You are free to go anywhere you please. I will not, however, return your goods, for God has given them to me. Go in peace and God will give you plenty more." Sarukhan was left speechless. Nāder then confiscated the belongings of all the Christian merchants. He appointed the Christian Manaysē, an Armenian by birth, to take care of all their living expenses while they were in Hamadān and to let them leave whenever they wished. The latter did as he was told and the Christian merchants, after several days, left for their own land.

---

[1] Text has the Persian term *abrīšam*.
[2] The term used is *kisa* (the Persian *kīse* or bags).
[3] Probably refers to *panzahr*, a kind of potion used as an antidote.
[4] Probably *yaşmak*, a kind of material for veils.
[5] Probably meaning "felt mats."
[6] *Lokum*, or Turkish delight.
[7] Possibly *sadra* meaning "vest."
[8] Probably *ǰalidqa* (*jaliqe-aba*), which means a waistcoat.
[9] Possibly *ruband* or *ruba* meaning "clothing."

Nāder stayed in Hamadān for about a month.[1] He then took some 15,000 soldiers and marched to take the city of Senne, which he did after seven days of fighting. Many wealthy Jews lived there. He seized them, subjected them to torture, and took 256 *tomans* from them. He also robbed those among the Turks who were rich. From some he took twenty, from others thirty, yet from others fifty, sixty, and as much as one hundred *tomans*, depending on their wealth. He then strongly chastised the Khan of Senne, who was called Sufan Vardi,[2] wanting to judged and execute him. Nāder asked, "When the Ottomans invaded our provinces, you were the governor. Why did you not come out with your forces and defend the land? Why did you surrender and cause the land such misery?" Heeding the petition of some of his advisors, however, Nāder spared Sufan Vardi's life in exchange for 3,000 *tomans*.

XII
How Nāder Took Tabriz from the Ottomans

Nāder then left some 2,000 men in the city of Senne for its defense, and with 18,000 soldiers marched on Tabriz. He reached a place which in the local dialect is called Saqqez[3] and is some six days' march from Tabriz. He camped there for three days. The Ottomans were informed that Nāder was approaching the city. Timur Pasha then went to the Pasha of Tabriz and said, "Nāder is marching against us and I hear that he is near. Let us take some of our troops, leave Tabriz, attack him in the open and scatter his forces before he has a chance to lay siege to the city." These words pleased the Pasha of Tabriz and he began to prepare a force.

While they were busy, Nāder, on the evening of the third day, organized his forces and crossed the distance of six days in one night and a day, arriving at noon. His speedy march spread defeat-

[1] MS A has *35 days*.

[2] Probably Sobḥān Vardi Khan, who became the Beglarbegi of Ardalān and who later rebelled against Nader.

[3] This town is 24 *farsaḵs* northwest of Senne.

ist notions among those who saw him before Tabriz. The Ottomans did not expect his sudden appearance, for they were sure he was six or seven days away. Nāder had crossed the distance in a day and a half. The Ottomans did not believe it was Nāder until he came near enough for them to recognize him. The Ottomans came out against him. They met near the village of Marand and the two armies faced each other. The Pasha of Tabriz, however, fled and took his troops. Timur Pasha and his 6,000 men remained alone in the fortress to face Nāder's 18,000 men. For seven days he fought and resisted the attacks of Nāder, for among Timur's troops were fierce fighters from Bosnia and Albania and other such people, some of whom had fled, while others remained. It is surprising, nevertheless, that he could resist for so many days, despite the fact that he had 6,000 against Nāder's 18,000.[1]Both sides suffered great casualties.

When Timur realized that out of 6,000 men, some 3,000 had been killed, he lost all hope of victory and began to think of a way to save his own life. He reviewed his troops and said to his *minbaşis*[2]"You can see that the Persians have more troops than we do. There is no way that we can hold the city with such small forces against the large Persian army. There is no point in holding out in the fortress, for whatever we do the city is lost. Why should we die for nothing? Let us leave the citadel and give battle. If we win we shall take the city, if we lose we shall flee to Erevan and save ourselves." The *minbaşis* approved. Timur left three hundred men in the citadel to guard it and came out with the remaining men to fight Nāder. He and his horse were covered in armor. He and his 2,800 men attacked Nāder's 18,000 troops. Four hours later his men were defeated and he, with some three hundred soldiers, fled to Erevan. He planned to overtake the Pasha of Tabriz and kill him for leaving him alone against Nāder, but the latter had slipped away.

---

[1]The last sentence does not appear in MS A.

[2]Officers in charge of 1,000 troops.

Nāder took Tabriz and killed all the Ottoman troops he found there. The Ottomans controlled the fortification in the center of town defended by two hundred men left by Timur, but Nāder razed it to its foundation and killed everyone. He remained in Tabriz for two months.[1]The Ottoman troops thus suffered defeat and they lost one city after another. The Sultan was not aware that his Grand Vizier, as noted, had ordered the surrender of these towns to the Persians, without his approval. He was under the impression that Tabriz, Hamadān, Senne, and Kermānshah were still in Turkish hands.

XIII[2]

How Nāder Took the Strongly-Fortified City of Herāt and How He Captured the Uzbek Bandit

While Nāder was gathering a 24,000-man army in Tabriz, with the intention of marching on Erevan, which is twelve-days' journey from Tabriz, news arrived from Ḵorāsān that the Afghans had gathered an army of 40,000 men in Herāt and were planning to move on Mašhad. Believing this rumor, Nāder postponed his march on Erevan and diverted his army to Mašhad. He arrived there 25 days later. After a few days in Mašhad, he reviewed his troops, and marched on Herāt, the main fort of the Afghans, who are known as great swordsmen and fierce fighters. Nāder camped near Herāt. The Afghans marched out to meet him. They fought for twelve days from dawn to dusk. The Afghans then locked themselves in the city and did not venture out for a while. Seven days later, the Afghans came out and fought the Persians for six days. They returned to the fortress and did not come out for forty-eight days. After that, they came out and fought for twenty-eight days.

---

[1]MS A has this line in the next chapter.

[2]The Erevan and Tbilisi editions have combined Chapters XIII-XVIII into Chapter VI with the following heading: *On Shah* Ṭahmāsp*'s Defeat by the Ottomans. How* Ṭahmāsp *was Deposed and the Infant Called 'Abbās Became Shah. The Autocracy of Nader and His Victories.*

They then took refuge in the fortress and stayed until the ninety-first day.[1]Herāt is a well-fortified town, with high walls, and could not be easily conquered.

At the conclusion of the ninety-first day of the siege, the food ran out and Herāt experienced a terrible famine. The hunger forced them to become cannibals. Nāder learned of the situation and ordered his men not to kill individual Afghans who came out of the fortress and approached the camp for food. The hunger soon forced more to come out and to obtain food from the camp. The troops of Nāder did not harm a single person. They were gently received and left alone. The town's people thus would come out of the fortress, enter the camp and leave at will. But when the commander of the Afghans finally appeared, he was seized and taken to Nāder. The latter received him with honor, presented him with a splendid *k̲al'at*, as a sign of respect, and sent him back to the fortress.[2]After that, all the defenders came out as well. With such prudence and deception Nāder conquered Herāt. He seized a large booty and with peaceable words and acts he brought the enemy to his side appointing a number of them as his military commanders. He did not take the population captive, nor did he devastate the town. However, he separated the inhabitants into groups and deported them to different Persian cities, some to Isfahan, others to Shiraz, and yet others to Mašhad. Although he did not force the Afghan soldiers to join him, some 7,000 came to him voluntarily. He appointed one of their khans as their governor. He then left Herāt for Mašhad and rested there.

In the meantime, in the land of the Uzbeks there rose a bandit who attacked many settlements and killed their people. The Uzbek king could not catch him. The bandit encroached over the boundary of Persian K̲orāsān. Learning that the man was a strong warrior who had eluded capture, and being appraised of the atrocities he had committed in various places, Nāder decided to seize him. When he heard that the bandit had crossed into K̲orāsān, Nāder

[1]MS B does not contain these four sentences.

[2]MS B has *kept him by his side.*

gathered a force of 3,000 young fighters and went after him. Hearing this, the bandit attacked him with 6,000 men. Nāder defeated him, slaughtered his men, captured him, and brought him to Mašhad. He kept him in jail for fifty-five[1] days and then he executed him. When the Uzbek king heard the news he was overjoyed.[2]

XIV

How The Ottoman Army Refused Peace With Persia and Resumed the War. How the Ottomans Defeated Shah Ṭahmāsp, Took Hamadān, and Concluded Peace.

Nāder then sent an envoy to the Uzbek king with the following message: "Send me 300,000 *tomans*[3] or else I shall invade you." The Uzbek king seized the envoy and put him in chains. When Nāder heard the news he began to prepare to march against him.[4]

Before continuing the current narrative, I have to give some details of what was going on with the Ottomans. Timur Pasha, who had fought at Tabriz and who had escaped to Erevan, got hold of the letter written by the Grand Vizier, 'Alī Pasha, to the governors. The letter stated, "Upon Nāder's approach, do not engage in battle, but surrender." Timur Pasha kept the letter, took it to Istanbul, and showed it to the Sultan. He listed the cities which the pashas had surrendered because of the note and denounced the Vizier to the Sultan. The Sultan, who had not been aware of this before, became furious and ordered the commander of the janissaries to execute the Vizier. A new minister was appointed in his place. When the subordinates of the Sultan, and especially the janissaries, heard of the Vizier's treachery, they began to grumble and told the Sultan,

[1]MS B has *50 days*.

[2]MS A does not contain this sentence.

[3]MS B has *1000 tomans*.

[4]The tribal leader was a Turkmen. Although nothing further is said in either manuscript, other sources mention that his expedition to Balkhan Dagh was not successful, see Lockhart, *Nadir Shah*, p. 61.

"We do not want to conclude peace with the Persians.[1] They have captured our kettle.[2] This is a great shame and dishonor, which we cannot tolerate. We wish to fight them and take it back." They then deposed the Sultan and put his brother, Mahmut,[3] in his place.[4]

The new Sultan[5] immediately sent three or four courtiers with a *farman* to the Pasha of Baghdad, Ahmet, which stated, "I appoint you as the commander-in-chief of all our forces and order you to march on Hamadān." After reading the order, Ahmet immediately gathered his troops in one place. His army consisted of 6,000 janissaries, 3,000 cavalry, 5,000 Arabs, 6,000 Kurds, 6,000 Bajilans, and many others from various lands. He ended with an impressively-prepared force of some 26,000 men. Taking all the necessary equipment and provisions, he marched on Hamadān. After six days he reached Zohāb; from there he proceeded to Kasri, then to Khana, from there to Kerend, from there to Harunābād, from there to Miyantash, from there to Kermānshah, from there to Behistun, from there to Senne, from there to Kangavar, from there to Sa'idabad.[6] Reaching Hamadān, he camped near the settlement of Laklār. He organized troop formations, built bastions, brought out his artillery and prepared to lay siege to the town with all possible haste.

Shah Ṭahmāsp, who was in Isfahan, was informed and marched to relieve Hamadān with his army of 100,000 men. He hoped to reach there before Ahmet Pasha had completed his siege of the city. In the meantime, Nāder, who was in Ḵorāsān watching the Afghans, learned of the Ottoman invasion. He wrote a letter to Shah Ṭahmāsp asking him not to commence an attack on the Ottomans, but to wait for his arrival, for he was aware of the Shah's

---

[1]Text has the Turkish term *acem* from the Arabic *'ajam*, meaning Persian.

[2]The term used is *kara kazan*, a black kettle, which was the symbol of the janissaries. To overturn the kettle was a sign of mutiny.

[3]Sultan Mahmut I (1730-1754). The addition in MS A does not have "brother." Mahmut was actually the nephew of Ahmet.

[4]This sentence is added by another hand in MS A and B.

[5]MS A has Sultan Ahmet.

[6]MS B does not contain this sentence.

cowardice.[1] The Shah ignored Nāder's advice, marched without delay and camped in a place called Red Hill.[2] The minute the Ottomans appeared on the battlefield, the Shah did not permit his troops to rest, but attacked the Ottomans head on. The two armies clashed and the field was covered with the blood of the fallen. Shah Ṭahmāsp's army took flight and lost 38,000 men. The Ottomans defeated the Persians. Realizing that even with superior forces he had not managed to defeat the Ottomans, the Shah fled to Isfahan. He then dispatched one of his khans, called Ma'yār, who was the chief of the armory,[3] as envoy to Ahmet Pasha, who was the commander-in-chief of the Ottoman army, to cede Hamadān and to negotiate a treaty of peace. Ahmet Pasha agreed, and having received Hamadān, put his seal on the treaty of peace. He left one of his commanders, who was called Ibrahim Ağa and who had led the right wing of his army,[4] as the governor of Hamadān and returned to Baghdad. Let us now return to Nāder.

XV

How Nāder Came to Isfahan, Tricked Shah Ṭahmāsp, Deposed Him and Sent Him to Ḵorāsān. How Nāder Made Ṭahmāsp's Infant Son Shah and Became the Defacto Ruler of Persia

Nāder, who was in Ḵorāsān, was fighting the 'Abdali Afghans, who had rebelled and were marching on Isfahan. Nāder cut off their passage to Isfahan and in a period of thirty-two days he totally routed the Afghans and returned to Ḵorāsān. When he learned of the Shah's behavior vis-à-vis the Ottomans and how, through his cowardice he had destroyed his army, had surrendered Hamadān into the hands of the Ottomans, and had signed a peace

---

[1] MS A does not contain this sentence.

[2] Text has the Turkish term *Kızıl Yokuş*. Abraham does not mention the first encounter with the Ottomans near Erevan, which forced the Shah's retreat to Tabriz and later to Hamadān.

[3] Text has the Turkish term *qūrčī bāşi.*

[4] Text has the Turkish term *sağkol ağasi.*

treaty with them, he became extremely furious. He sought ways to catch the Shah and put him into confinement, so that he alone would be in charge of the State. For he realized that that effeminate man was ill-intentioned and cowardly, that all his actions and thoughts were for the destruction of the State and not for its well-being. Nāder therefore gathered a large force and prepared to march on Isfahan.[1]His army consisted of 48,000 cavalry and 6,000 infantry. He provided them with heavy armor and various weapons, and leaving Ḵorāsān, he and his entire army moved on Isfahan. Thirty-eight days later, he reached the capital. He did not enter the town, however, but camped outside it, on an open plain called Ašrafābād.

Even before Nāder had reached Isfahan, some of the great Persian nobles told the Shah, "May God grant you a long life! Nāder is coming here with evil intent. We have ascertained that all his actions and moves are insidious. He plans to grab you and take your throne away from you. Are you aware with how many troops is he coming? Why does he have to come with so many men, if his intentions are peaceful?" The Shah's advisors continued to make similar speeches, but he did not believe them. Among the notables, there was a Christian, an Armenian by birth, who was called Dawit' Beg and who was a very wise advisor. Well aware of Nāder's machinations and fearing the great misfortunes that would befall the Shah and his throne, he secretly got through to the Shah's private quarters three days later. He came at night and without anyone present said in a sympathetic and friendly manner, "My liege and sovereign lord, beware. Nāder is coming like an enemy with evil intentions. I am positive that he is coming to capture you, put you in chains, and take your throne for himself. He will arrive any day now. Watch out and be on your guard against him." All of a sudden the Shah became wary and he began to think. His mind was troubled, his heart was filled with worry, sleep escaped him, and he lay awake that entire night. At daybreak he summoned all his notables to court and together they decided on strict meas-

[1]These last four sentences are absent from MS A.

ures. The Shah and all his 23,000 available troops prepared for war. They decided to come out from behind the walls of Isfahan and meet Nāder, who was approaching the city with his 54,000 well-armed men. This accomplished, Shah Ṭahmāsp was at first prepared not to trust Nāder, but later, as we shall see, he was deceived by Nāder's servile flattery.[1]

When Nāder reached Isfahan and pitched camp in the vicinity of the town, he learned about the Shah's preparations. He began to suspect that the Shah was aware of his plan. He got off his horse, and on foot, accompanied by several of his military commanders, went to pay his salutations. He prostrated himself at the Shah's feet and with humility and devotion he bowed before him, stating, "Your Majesty, for what reason are you here in the open? Is it possible that you have heard some slanderous accusations against me and doubt my devotion towards you? If that is so, do not believe it, for such talk comes from the enemy. I am the same person who from the very beginning has served Your Majesty honestly and has carried out all your orders. I have gone everywhere you have sent me and have fought everyone you ordered me to. I am now at your feet. I shall not act without your express order. If you order me to go to Ḵorāsān, I shall go to Ḵorāsān; if to Qazvīn, I shall go to Qazvīn. If you order me to go against the Ottomans, I shall attack the Ottomans. Whatever you command, I, your servant, will carry it out." With many such false, servile, and flattering utterances and assurances, he finally dispelled the Shah's suspicions, gained his trust, and convinced him to return to Isfahan.

Upon returning to the city, the Shah summoned Nāder, showered him with honors, and put him above many other notables. He then said, "Bring all your troops into the city. You and your army should be inside Isfahan and not outside its walls." Nāder answered, "I am prepared to carry out my Sovereign's order, but if I bring my entire army into the city, they may harass the population." Concealing his real motives in such sweet words, he swayed the Shah. The Shah said, "Very well, do not bring the army into Is-

---

[1]This paragraph appears in a much-condensed form in MS A.

fahan. Let them stay outside the gates." Thus Nāder's army remained camped by the city. After that, Nāder acted with feigned humility and flattery and turned the Shah's disposition into believing that he was his trusted and obedient friend. The Shah soon transferred all his authority, the affairs of State, and the command of the army into Nāder's hands. He told his courtiers, "Whatever Nāder does is by our command and to our benefit." He told Nāder, "Do whatever you think is right and nothing else. In particular do not break the peace that I have concluded with the Ottomans, for it is not proper to break a king's word." Nāder replied, "I shall always act according to the wishes of my Lord."

Nāder then began to inspect his army and check on his commanders to ascertain if anyone had deserted and if their numbers had been reduced. He also inspected the Shah's army, taking its strength and numbers into consideration. He did this often, each time noting the number of both armies. The Shah remained silent, did not forbid it, and even stated, "Whatever he does, he does for our benefit." The cunning Khan then began to dispatch the Shah's soldiers here and there. Six thousand of them he sent to Tabriz, five thousand to Qazvīn, two thousand to Mazandarān. He thus dispatched all the rest of the best-prepared units of the Shah's army to various locations. He visited the Shah often and by continuous flattery and feigned love he won the Shah's heart.

One day the Shah honored Nāder with a banquet. Six days later, Nāder took the liberty to invite the Shah to a feast in his quarters. He had previously spread the rumor that he planned to return to K̲orāsān and he now begged the Shah to come to a farewell banquet, stating, "I have to depart to my home. Prior to my departure I beg Your Majesty, my Master and my Sovereign, to grant me, his servant, the great favor to set aside your fastidiousness and to attend the banquet, which I, your servant, in my poverty have prepared for you. I can receive no higher honor or glory than your presence and merrymaking in my poor tent." The Shah accepted his invitation and went to the banquet. Nāder prepared a sumptuous feast under his roof, worthy of a great king.

During the banquet, while they were enjoying the food and the Shah was in a good mood, Nāder said, "I wish that my Master and Sovereign would grant his servant a favor." The Shah replied, "Ask and it shall be granted." Nāder said, "My Sovereign, I have heard you say that you partake wine. Therefore, if Your Highness permits it I shall order some wine be brought to the table to increase our happiness." The Shah replied, "You are right, let them bring wine." Nāder sent men to the Armenians in Jugha (New Julfa)[1] and they brought twenty to thirty flagons[2] of wine from the house of Kalantar[3] Hovhannēs. They began to eat and drink and have a merry time late into the night. The Shah was very cheerful and he drank a great deal of wine. He became drunk and began to nod. At midnight, Nāder went out and told the Shah's bodyguards, "You go to sleep now, the Shah is already asleep." The Shah, who was in a terrible state of drunkenness and unconsciousness, was alone in the room.

When the Shah's bodyguards went to sleep in their quarters, the crafty[4] Nāder entered alone into the room and slapped[5] the Shah's face, as they do to children. He grabbed him and tied him with a rope. He then called three to four strong men from his own troops, and they tied him further and put his feet in shackles. They threw him in a room and kept him in confinement. At daybreak, Nāder arrested all the advisers of the Shah, before they had a chance to discover what he had done, and had their heads cut off.

After that, he entered the Shah's living quarters and took his wife, his sister, his mother, his relatives, and other women who

---

[1]The Armenian district across the Zayandeh River (on the other side of Isfahan), constructed by Shah 'Abbās I for the Armenians of Julfa in Nakhichevan whom he forcibly brought to his capital, see Bournoutian, "The Armenian Community of Isfahan in the Seventeenth Century," *Armenian Review* 24-25 (1971-1972), 27-45, 33-50.

[2]The term used is *shusha* (from the Persian *šīše*, which means "glass" and "bottles").

[3]The *Kalantar* was an official who performed the duties of mayor. He was the secular leader of the Armenians of New Julfa.

[4]This adjective does not appear in MS A.

[5]The term used is *sili* (from the Persian *sīle*).

were in the household. He took the Shah's sister as his wife and the Shah's wives became his concubines. Nāder took all the Shah's property. He sent the Shah and his mother to Ḵorāsān. When Nāder ordered their departure to Ḵorāsān, the citizens, who saw the Shah and his mother in chains, became confused, fell into deep mourning, and shed tears. But no one could come to his aid and rescue him from his enemies. After sending the Shah to Ḵorāsān, Nāder settled in Isfahan and began to rule in his place.

A few days later, Nāder summoned all his military commanders and most of his units and told them, "Do you know why I have summoned you?" They answered, "We do not know, but we are prepared to carry out any of our master's orders." Nāder then said, "I have summoned you to inform you that in place of the Shah, who was sent to Ḵorāsān, we have put his son on the throne. We have ordered that all coins[1] within the Persian realm be minted bearing his name. We shall conduct all the affairs of State and shall go to war in his name, for his birth sign is charmed and he is born under a lucky star."[2] The son who he proposed to make king, however, was a six month-old suckling child, called 'Abbās.[3] With the approval of the army, Nāder declared the baby as the new Shah[4] and sent him to be reared in Qazvīn. Nāder told them that the Shah was a drunkard[5] and a sodomite[6] and could not govern. He added, "I sent him to Ḵorāsān to bring him to his senses." In this way, he clearly managed to gain the support of the army and the population and to calm their fears. Thus, instead of anxiety and outcry, the people loved him, praised his wisdom, and commended to him their own wellbeing.

---

[1]The term used is the Persian word *sekke*, which means "coin."

[2]The term used, half Armenian and half Perso-Arabic, is *lav baḵt* (good fortune).

[3]'Abbās III was actually 8 months old.

[4]The investiture occurred on 7 September 1732 with Nāder as regent.

[5]Term used is the Persian word *ḵomār* for "tipsy."

[6]Term used is the Persian word *loṭī* (from the Biblical Lot).

XVI

How Nāder Angered the Baḵtiyārīs by His Behavior Toward Shah Ṭahmāsp. How They Rose Against Nāder, Elected Their Own King, and Marched on Isfahan. How Nāder Went to Crush Them and How They Sought Refuge in a Fort. How Nāder Left Them and Crossing a Large River Marched on the Ottomans in Baghdad

The Baḵtīyāri[1]tribesmen, who became aware of Nāder's behavior towards Shah Ṭahmāsp, gathered in a place and chose one of their own leaders as shah. They gathered an army and marched to Isfahan to avenge the deposed monarch. Reaching the suburbs of Isfahan, they looted six or seven villages and enslaved their people. They soon devastated 113[2]settlements in the region. Hearing this, Nāder marched against them with a large force. He first went to a place called Ganduman.[3]From there he proceeded to Dasgerd[4]and continued to Ferendgān, entering the Baḵtīyāri territory. The Baḵtīyāris fled to a fortress called Jumlan,[5]settled in and did not venture out. The fortress was very secure. The river called Ab-e Kuran flowed on one side, while a steep mountain, which was very difficult to ascend, guarded the other side of the fort. Realizing this, Nāder bypassed the fort and moved towards the Hovizeh province, which was populated by Arabs, Lor, Ḵārejī,[6]Shi'is, and

---

[1]One of the largest tribal confederations in Persia, the Baḵtīyāris inhabit a large region located in the central part of the Zagros Mountains. They speak a Lori dialect, for more detils see G. R. Garthwaite, *Khans and Shahs. A Documentary Analysis of the Bakhtiyari in Iran* (Cambridge, 1983).

[2]MS B has 97 villages.

[3]A district (*mahal*) of the Isfahan province, west of Rar.

[4]Also called Dastjerd, on the Isfahan-Kašān road.

[5]Lockhart calls the stronghold Banavar, *Nadir Shah*, p. 65. It may possibly be the present-day J̌umleqan.

[6]A primary Persian source refers to them as those who follow the *ḵārejī* religion, *'Alam Ārā-ye Nāderī*, pp. 1173-1174. The text does not make it clear if they were members of the earliest Islamic sect known as the *Ḵhwariḏjites*. The term is also used to refer to Arab tribesmen.

other groups.[1] The moment the governor of Hovizeh, who was called ‘Alī Mardān Khan, heard of Nāder’s approach, he hastened to meet him and greeted him with fabulous gifts[2] and great honor. Nāder received him well, presented him with a magnificent *k̲al‘at*, appointed him as commander of the army, and ordered him to attack the Bak̲tīyāris.

Meanwhile, Nāder proceeded to Kermānshah via K̲orramābād[3] and K̲azal, where he rested for thirty-eight days[4] while assessing the strength of his forces. He then moved on Baghdad and reached Miyantash. He then advanced to Harunābād, moved on to Kerend and finally to Kiukoṛ,[5] which, in the language of the Kurds means “mountain of the boys,” for it is difficult to ascend and old men cannot climb it. Four hours after leaving Kiukoṛ, Nāder observed that the road was devoid of human traffic. The reason for this was that the mountain pass served as a border between the Ottoman Empire and Persia. A single road traversed the pass. A caravansary called Khuna’i Mehmun[6] by the Kurds was located there. Nāder was informed that the Ottoman army was stationed by that caravansary, which was three hours away. At midnight, Nāder advanced. He ordered his troops not to go by the afore-mentioned road. Rather, leading his horse, he climbed the mountain on foot with his troops behind him. They thus crossed the mountain, caught the Ottomans offguard and attacked their post half an hour before sunrise.

They moved on to Zohāb, whose governor was called Ahmet Bek. The latter was not prepared, for he did not know that Nāder

---

[1]A Persian primary source differs. It states that after a 21-day siege the Bak̲tīyāris made a sortie and were annihilated, see Lockhart, *Nadir Shah*, p. 65.

[2]The text has the Persian term *pīškeš*, which is a magnificent gift given to a prince as a tribute.

[3]There are four such settlements in the Hamadān-Kermānshah region. The text does not specify which of these was on Nāder’s route.

[4]MS B has *30 days*.

[5]The Kurdish terms are *kiu* (mountain) and *korre* (meaning boy or son). Its present-day name is Kuh-e Korreh Mīyāne, near the village of Mīyāne, 8 *farsak̲s* (*farsang*, equal to 18,000 feet) west of Sanandaǰ.

[6]Perso-Kurdish term which translates as “guest house.”

had crossed the border, without the knowledge of the frontier guards. Thus when he saw that Nāder had suddenly appeared before Zohāb, he rushed out with a force of 6,000 men and gave battle. The struggle lasted from daybreak until noon. Ahmet Bek's army was defeated and he took flight. A certain Qāǰār tribesman, however, pursued him, overtook him after an hour, and shot an arrow which struck Ahmet Bek's helmet [and unhorsed him]. He caught Ahmet Bek and took him to Nāder. He received a reward of 113 *tomans*.

Nāder spent six days in Zohāb and then moved on Baghdad. After a three-hour march they reached a river called Zangane. The river, at the time, had risen and had overflowed its banks. Nāder halted for two hours and conferred with his commanders as to the feasibility of crossing the river. He then addressed his cavalry with the following words, "Whoever is devoted to me will follow me and will cross the river on horseback." With these words he was first to dash into the water and to reach the other side of the river. His 48,000 horsemen were so inspired that they all drove into the river after him and crossed to the other bank. Some one hundred of his horsemen drowned in the river. The 6,000 infantrymen remained on the other bank. Nāder ordered thick chains of iron to be firmly fixed on both banks. Swimmers took twelve chains across the river, tied them together, and formed four cables. Wooden planks were then placed on top of these cables and earth was poured on them. A road was thus created and the entire infantry passed to the other side. After that they dragged their cannons and other equipment over that bridge. Although Nāder had planned to advance toward Baghdad, he changed his mind and marched on Kirkuk. He came upon the village of Tabalu, which was a pleasant place, but its people had fled to Kirkuk.

When they reached the prosperous village of Lailān, its inhabitants greeted them with great humility, for they were Shi'i, or of the same religion as the Persians. Nāder called the village elders and asked, "Do you know why have I summoned you?" They replied, "No." Nāder said, "I need three of your men, who know the road to Baghdad. They shall serve as our guides." The *ta-*

nuter,[1] who was called Kekhya[2] Qāsem in their language, and who had been their *kadḵodā*[3] for seven years, arrived. Nāder gave him a *ḵal'at* and other gifts. Qāsem then guided the Persian army. Upon exiting Lailān, Nāder took the road to Baghdad and reached Kara Täppä, where he pitched his camp. Eight days later, he moved on Ǧaẕārabāṭ, which he found abandoned, for its inhabitants had fled to Baghdad. The reason that Nāder altered his route from one direction to the other was to force the Ottomans to come out from their forts and meet him in battle. None, however, came out to fight him in the open. From Ǧaẕārabāṭ he reached Mandali, some of whose inhabitants were Shi'i, some Sunni. The Sunnis had fled to Baghdad, but the Shi'is had remained. Nāder stayed there for twelve days and then moved on to Ḥilla. Before reaching Ḥilla, two Persian armies, numbering 30,000 and led by 'Alī Mardān Khan and Bābā Khan of Ḵorramābād, joined him in accordance with his prior orders. He then did not advance to Ḥilla himself, but dispatched the newly arrived forces there.

XVII

How Nāder Moved on Baghdad, Fought Osman Pasha, Was Defeated and Retreated to Hamadān

Nāder stayed in Mandali for seven days and then moved on Baghdad. He pitched camp in a place called Imam 'Ażam, which is similar to our saints' shrines, an hour or two away from the city. Many Muslim sheikhs, who had a good reputation among the population and who knew the law and the holy scriptures, resided in that region. Nāder gave them *ḵal'ats* and treated them with great respect. They, in turn, showed their enthusiasm and love for him and wrote to the sheikhs, who are the Muslim equivalent of priests, of the shrines of Imam'Alī, Imam Mūsā, Imam Bāqer, Imam

---

[1] Armenian term for "village elder."

[2] "Village elder" in the Erevani dialect.

[3] Persian term for "village elder."

Kāżem, Imam 'Abbās, Imam Zenal, and Imam Zeynab. They praised Nāder in these letters and encouraged their fellow-preachers to submit to Nāder, citing the great honors he had bestowed on them. Hearing this, they and their followers gladly submitted to Nāder. Nāder was now informed that 'Ali Mardān Khan and Bābā Khan, whom he had dispatched to take Ḥilla, had taken it. They were now planning to cross the Shat River[1] and advance toward the shrines of Imam 'Alī or Imam Mūsā. Nāder immediately wrote the following note to them, "Do not go there, for they have already submitted to us." They then changed course and marched on Baghdad, which was on the other side of the Tigris River. After crossing it, they slaughtered numerous Ottomans and Arabs, so that the entire field was filled with corpses and blood covered the earth. It was hot and humid and the stench of the dead was so strong that no one dared pass that place. Bābā Khan then pitched his camp in a place which the locals called Karşu-Yaka,[2] for it is located by a large settlement on the other bank of the river, which flows in front of Baghdad and faces the Cizir[3] Gate.[4] It had a bridge over it, which is connected by two thick chains, for passage into and out of the city

Thus Bābā Khan and 'Alī Mardān Khan laid siege to Baghdad from one side and Nāder from the other. They did not attack the city, since, wanting to move swiftly, Nāder had not brought any cannons. After laying siege to the city for forty-eight days,[5] Nāder received the twenty-five cannons that he had left behind in Zohāb. They began to place the cannons and to fire on the city. Both sides exchanged cannon fire. Since the Ottoman cannons were larger than Nāder's, they were capable of hurtling larger cannon balls. One particular cannon, the largest, could hurl a cannon ball filled

---

[1]The Shat (or *Šat al-Arab*) is formed from the Tigris and the Euphrates Rivers at Basra and flows into the Persian Gulf.

[2]From the Turkish words *qarsu* (*karsu*), meaning opposite, and *yaqa* (*yaka*), meaning shore.

[3]From the Turkish *ciz*, a wooden beam or log, in this case bridge.

[4]Text has the Turkish term *kapusi*, which translates as "gate."

[5]MS B has *40 days*.

with approximately forty *okha*[1] of gunpowder. Although Nāder's forces were not concentrated in one area, such a cannon ball was fired from the fort. It exploded in the middle of the camp and killed one hundred troops. Seeing such casualties, Nāder moved the front further back. After that, the Ottoman cannon balls could not harm his troops, but neither could his cannon balls reach Baghdad. Thus they faced each other for fifty-five days without firing their artillery. The Ottomans then fired the large cannon once again, but the explosion damaged a wall of the fortifications and destroyed many houses, after which the Turks did not use it again. After fifty-five days of siege, the Ottomans, fully armed, made a sudden sortie with the intention of attacking the Persians. They were divided into two groups and exited through two different gates: The White Gate[2] and the Imam 'Ażam Gate. Twenty-four thousand men came out of the White Gate and ten thousand from the Imam 'Ażam Gate. The Pasha, however, remained in the city and did not permit the citizens to leave either, for half of them were Persians[3] and he suspected that they would join the troops of Nāder.

The minute Nāder saw that the Ottomans had attacked him, he moved his troops forward without his cannons. The Ottomans, who had brought ten loaded cannons with them, began to fire on the Persian forces. Nāder then divided his troops into four groups so that he would not subject his entire army to the cannon fire. Having used their guns, the Ottomans could not reload their cannons fast enough, and while they were busy reloading, the Persians fell on them from four sides and stopped the enemy from using its firepower. The two armies clashed and began to slaughter each other with swords and muskets for some seven hours. Eight thousand Ottomans and six thousand Persians perished. The Ottoman army suffered a defeat and fled back into the fortress and did not venture out again.

Nāder pitched his camp and laid siege to the city for eight-eight days. The city was faced with such a famine that an *okha* of dog

---

[1] One *okha* equals 1.2 kg. MS B has 80 liters, which equals 36 lbs.
[2] Text has the Turkish term *Aq Kapu*.
[3] Abraham probably means Shi'is.

meat cost forty *marchil*,[1] and even then it was hard to come by. Nāder sent a number of detachments toward Mosul, where they devastated villages and towns, killed the men and enslaved the women and children. They did not reach Mosul, however, for they lacked sufficient troops. Having reached a place that the local people called Hazrat Yonuz,[2] after the prophet John, they turned back.

Nine months after the start of the siege, the Ottoman sultan, Mahmut, dipatched Topal[3] Osman Pasha with 250,000 troops to Baghdad. Hearing that Topal Pasha had reached Mosul, Nāder sent envoys to Baghdad to discuss terms of peace. He wrote to Ahmet Pasha, the commander of Baghdad, "Surrender the city and we shall conclude a peace." Ahmet Pasha responded, "Do not ask for the fortress? Come and fight with our troops, and if you defeat us, then you shall have it." When Topal Osman approached Baghdad, Nāder left 6,000 troops to continue the siege and together with the rest of his army he went to meet Osman Pasha.

Topal Osman hurried and took possession of the river, so that Nāder was not able to reach it in time to gain access to water. Upon Nāder's approach, Topal Osman dug in and prepared to meet him with his entire army. He had some 105 cannons, while Nāder had not brought any. Nāder prepared his troops for an immediate attack on the Turks. He brought forth 12,000 troops armed with muskets, followed by troops with other weapons. The two armies clashed and at first Nāder's forces were victorious over the Ottomans, forcing them to flee towards the river. The river was, however, separated by a large depression, where the Ottomans had fortified and from where they successfully fired on the Persian troops, who were totally exposed from all sides. Bullets rained on the Persians and found their marks, while the Persians could not see the Ottomans, who were hidden in the ravine. Not a single Persian bullet found its mark. The Persian troops began to suffer from thirst, but there was no water, for as stated before, the Ottoman

---

[1] A silver coin worth over half a gold ruble.

[2] Translates as "Saint John."

[3] The text refers to him as Osman Pasha the Lame (Topal means "lame" or crippled in Turkish), hereinafter Topal Osman Pasha.

troops had, upon their arrival in Baghdad, gained access to the river, while the Persians did not manage to reach it in time. Nāder permitted his advance guard, that is, those who were armed with muskets, to seek water, which was about half an hour's distance from the front. The janissaries, led by Mamish Pasha, Rustam Pasha and Husein Pasha, then emerged from their fortifications[1] and showered the remaining Persian troops with a thick hail of bullets, forcing them to disperse and flee. Although some of the cavalry survived, all the infantrymen perished. The reason for this disaster was not only the lack of water, but an hour or two after the commencement of the battle, a strong wind blew dust, powder-smoke and sand in the direction of the Persians, which choked and blinded them. The heat, which was especially severe in that region, also scorched them. The summer in that province is so hot that, according to witnesses, clothes can ignite without the use of fire.[2] Nāder's troops were scattered in all directions. Some fled to Mandali, others to Ǧaẕārabāṭ, and others to Zohāb. Nāder himself fled and his troops did not know if he was alive or dead.[3]

There were six Armenians among the Persian army, who had the rank of *yüzbaşi*[4] and commanded one hundred men each. They were: Dawit`, who was known as Gorēts'its'i Beg; Geghak'un Abidjan son of Adovm of Sot'; Aydin Bek Aghajan of Ch'abnets'; Balig son of Movses of Ch'abnets'; and Haghnazar, son of Topuz Chadakereants'. They had five hundred men with them.[5] Haghnazar accompanied Nāder in his flight. The rest fled to Zohāb. A certain Persian commander, called J̌ān, who was the son of Moḥammad 'Alī of Isfahan, was in Zohāb and told the Armenians, "Stay here and do not leave. We shall attack the Ottomans together." The Armenians refused and said, "No one will force us to go back and

[1] Text has the Persian term *matares*, from *matrez*, meaning "bastion."

[2] The battle, according to other primary sources, took place on 19 July 1733.

[3] MS A differs from MS B in the order of the sentences in this paragraph.

[4] Officer in charge of 100 men.

[5] Both manuscripts name only five *yüzbaşis* (with a total of 500 men) and not six.

fight the Ottomans." They did not stay, but left for Kermānshah and Hamadān.

News arrived that Nāder had reached Hamadān and that the governor of that city had ordered celebrations. Meanwhile, Nāder had put officers at the crossroads to gather the men who had fled and to assemble them. Those who were spared the sword were gathered together and brought to Nāder. After inspecting his army, Nāder realized that the six [Armenian] commanders had survived. They were brought to Nāder.[1] He said, "I brought you to fight and not to flee." He then ordered their heads cut off.[2] He then ordered the execution of 152 notables[3] who had fled the battlefield. Three days later, he reorganized his army and appointing six or seven khans in place of the dead officers. From the 92,000-strong army, only 15,000 had remained.

XVIII

How Nāder Once Again Moved Towards Baghdad to Battle Topal Osman Pasha. How He Routed the Turks and Killed Topal Osman. How He Concluded Peace With the Governor of Baghdad. How He Attacked the Baḵtiyārīs, Killed Many, and Exiled 48,000 Households to Ḵorāsān

Nāder prepared his 15,000-man army to do battle once again with Topal Osman Pasha. Meanwhile, Topal Osman, after defeating Nāder, wrote to Ahmet Pasha of Baghdad stating, "You have been hiding in Baghdad for nine months. Come out and face the Persians." Ahmet Pasha replied, "You have not fought the main Persian army. They will soon arrive. I am afraid to come out."

Let us now return to Nāder, who after sixty days left Hamadān. He marched and covered the fifteen days' route to Zohāb in seven. From there, after a three-days' forced march, he arrived in Kirkuk.

---

[1]According to the text, one of the commanders had remained with Nāder, so only five must have been brought to him.

[2]This episode is not recorded in MS B.

[3]MS A has *112 officers*.

To catch them off-guard,[1] he circled the foot of a mountain and descended upon the camp of Osman Pasha at dawn, when most of the troops were asleep and unprepared for battle. The enemy camp was filled with alarm and he [Nāder] struck them down, seized Osman Pasha, cut off his head and sent it to Ahmet Pasha in Baghdad. Nāder's army killed more than 45,000[2] Ottoman soldiers and forced the rest to flee.

After that, Nāder marched on Baghdad. On arrival he did not do battle but concluded a brotherly alliance with the governor of that city, Ahmet Pasha. He declared that he was pleased with the loyalty displayed by the Pasha to his Sultan. During his discussions with Ahmet Pasha, Nāder stated, "My heart is full of admiration for your perseverance. I laid siege to this city for nine months, forced you to suffer from hunger and face the sword, but you did not surrender the fortress and remained obedient to your liege. From now on, therefore, there shall be no enmity between us, rather brotherly love will bond us until death."[3]

After that, Nāder went to Hovizeh. He took 'Alī Mardān Khan and Bābā Khan with him and went to battle the Baḵtiyārīs. The Baḵtiyārīs, having learned of Nāder's initial defeat, had once again rebelled and had appointed one of their leaders, called 'Alī, as their shah. They had gathered a force and were preparing to march on Isfahan and gain their independence. Nāder possessed no more than 15,000 troops. For although he had started with 92,000, during his first encounter with the Ottomans, as stated above, he had lost many men and his army had been reduced to 15,000. 'Alī Mardān Khan and Bābā Khan, however, had 30,000 troops at their disposal. Nāder added them to his army and ended with 45,000 men. He entered the Baḵtiyārī territory and went to a place called Jumlan. For eighteen days the Baḵtiyārīs and Nāder's forces engaged in battle. Nāder's army overcame the Baḵtiyārīs and killed so many that, as they say, rivers of blood flowed on the plain. Nāder captured the rest of their army, took their city and carried its

[1]Text has *ğāfel*.
[2]MS B has *three times the number of his own troops*.
[3]MS A has this in another part of the chapter.

inhabitants into captivity. Forty-eight thousand households were sent to Ḵorāsān, which is also called Mašhad. He did not settle them in one place, however. He divided them into groups; three hundred households he settled in one town, four hundred households in another, two hundred somewhere else, and the rest in various other settlements. Three hundred were entrusted to the Armenians of New Julfa, who took care of them for two months before dispatching them to Shiraz.

After that, Nāder marched on Shiraz, whose governor, called Moḥammad,[1] had rebelled against him, even though Nāder had appointed him to control the disloyal Balūč. Instead of convincing the Balūč to become loyal to Nāder, Moḥammad rose against Nāder, gathered an army, and planned to march on Isfahan. Meanwhile, he had gone to the Bandar region[2] and had killed those who had refused to join him. He added the rest to his army, went to Shiraz and prepared to attack Isfahan.

Nāder was informed of Moḥammad's intentions and dispatched an envoy with a letter that stated, "What are you doing? You are my servant and have eaten my bread. I raised you above five or six other khans. What is the reason that you have rebelled, have become alienated, have raised your sword and men against me? Repent and change your evil ways." Nāder sent similar messages three times, but the latter did not answer. After the fourth message, Moḥammad Khan replied, "I risk my neck on my action. Let God decide between us. Be aware that either I or you shall lose our life."

When Nāder heard this, he no longer communicated with Moḥammad Khan. Instead, he gathered his army and marched on Shiraz. Moḥammad Khan was informed of his approach and went out to meet him on the plain. During the battle Moḥammad's army took flight and many were killed. He himself barely escaped and

---

[1]This is the same Moḥammad Khan Balūč, the former envoy to Istanbul (see Chapter IX.

[2]Although Bandar signifies Bandar ʻAbbās, the meaning here implies the Persian Gulf coast.

took refuge in a fortress in the Bandar region called ‘Avaż.[1] The chief of the fortress, a certain Sheikh Jabbār, had an extraordinary knowledge of the supernatural and the Muslims of the region considered him a saint and believed his every word, for he had reportedly performed many miracles. Moḥammad Khan thus went to the Sheikh, told him what had occurred, and begged him for God's sake to intercede on his behalf with Nāder, since the latter held the Sheikh in great reverence.

The Sheikh gave in to his request and sent a letter to Nāder stating, "For my sake, receive Moḥammad Khan, who has repented and who wishes to return to your bosom. Have mercy on him, do not execute him, although he is not worthy of your generosity." Nāder responded, "Let it be so. Because of your entreaties I shall not execute him. Send him to us." The Sheikh showed Nāder's letter to Moḥammad Khan and the latter went to him. When he appeared before him, Nāder said, "Do you remember when I was in Baghdad and wrote to you not to go against me? You answered that God shall decide which one of us will remain alive. Well, God has placed you in my hands and it is just that I should kill you." Moḥammad Khan replied, "Do as you wish; I am here in your hands." Nāder answered, "Although you deserve to die, for the sake of the Sheikh who begged that I spare your life, I shall spare you. But I shall give you a minor punishment." He then ordered one of his slaves[2] to remove Moḥammad Khan's eyes. Nāder then gave the blind khan one hundred *tomans* and said, "Go! Live on this sum and pray for me." He entrusted him to fifteen soldiers and sent him to Mašhad.[3] He then went to Isfahan to prepare the conquest of Shirvan and Shemakhi.

This is the end of my history. Nothing else remains. I have written what I saw with my own eyes and what I recall from 1173 (1724) to 1183 (1734), which transpired between the Ottomans and the Persians. I, Abraham of Erevan, son of Hovhannēs, have composed this narrative. If a Christian reads this, let him say a prayer

[1] It is located close to Bushire.
[2] Text has *ğūlām*.
[3] Persian sources have him dying under torture in Isfahan.

for my father, Hovhannēs, my mother, Maryam, my sister Darda Khat'un, my sister Shahum, my brother Constantine, my brother Karagoz, my brother Adi Bek, my brother Filomen, my brother Petros, and my brother P'anos. My father, mother, and brothers were all martyred in the hands of the Ottomans.[1] Whoever prays for them shall perform his duty to Christ. Amen.[2]

XIX[3]

How The Envoys From Moscovy Arrived in Isfahan and Demanded the Tribute Agreed to by Shah Ṭahmāsp and Nāder's Stern Reply. How Nāder Marched on and Captured Erevan from the Ottomans and How He Demanded Payment from the Persian and Armenian Residents of Erevan

After completing his preparations, Nāder marched on Shemakhi and Shirvan.[4] In order to detail the events that took place, it is necessary to explain what had occurred previously.

During the time when Shah Ṭahmāsp regained Isfahan from the Afghan ruler, Gīlān was in the hands of Muscovy. When Shah Ṭahmāsp returned to Isfahan, he dispatched envoys to the Ottoman Sultan with a letter, which stated, "Return my cities, which you took during the Afghan invasion, back to me. For I, with God's grace, have now defeated the Afghans, have removed them from Persia, and have ascended the royal throne of my father." The Ot-

---

[1]His sisters were probably enslaved by the Turks.

[2]This paragraph does not appear in MS B. The text is in the form of a colophon. It is placed on folio 70b instead of at the end of MS A. Since the size of the folios changes beginning with folio 71a, it seems that Abraham must have decided to continue his narrative.

[3]The Erevan and Tbilisi editions have combined Chapters XIX-XXI into Chapter VII under the heading: *Nāder's Campaign in Armenia, Georgia, the Land of the Albanians, and the Land of the Lesghians. The Defeat of the Ottoman Army. The Gathering at the Moğān Steppe and How Nāder Became the Shah of the Persians.*

[4]Although Abraham seems to view the two as separate entities, Shemakhi was the main city of the Shirvan province.

toman Sultan replied in these words, "First you have to retake Gīlān from the Moscovites and then you may ask us. That is if you think you have the right to do so." The Shah then sent an envoy with a message to the Tsar of Russia requesting the return of Gīlān. He received the following answer, "I have spent large sums and used many soldiers[1] in conquering and defending the towns of the Gīlān Province. I am prepared to return them to you if you compensate me for the expenses[2] which I have incurred up to now, as well as an interest of 80,000 *tomans* per annum." Shah Ṭahmāsp said[3] he would pay the sum and Moscovy evacuated Gīlān, returned to its own borders, and concluded a peace treaty[4] with the Persians, by which the Shah had to pay an annual sum of 80,000 *tomans*.

A year later, when the deadline for the payment of the aforementioned sum arrived, Moscovy sent an envoy to Persia and demanded the money from the Shah. The envoy was Simēon, son of Abraham,[5] an Armenian from Erzerum.[6] When he arrived in Isfahan, he realized that the Shah was no longer in power, for he had been deposed by Nāder and sent to Ḵorāsān in chains. Since there was no one who could respond to his mission, he became worried. Nāder, however, summoned him and asked, "Where are you from and why did you come here?" Simēon answered, " I am the envoy of the Tsar of Moscovy and I have brought a message for the Shah." Nāder said, "Give me the letter so that I can ascertain what the Tsar wants from our Shah." Simēon replied, "I cannot do that. The letter is addressed to the Shah. I was ordered to present it to him and not to you." Nāder answered, "In that case stay here awhile until I conclude the war with the Afghans who have risen against us. On my return I shall give you my answer." He then assigned living-quarters for the envoy and went to war.

---

[1] Text has the Russian and European term *soldat*.
[2] Text has the Persian term *ḵarǰ* (meaning "to spend" or "expenses").
[3] Text has the Persian term *qā'el* (meaning "unaware").
[4] The Treaty of Rašt (1 February 1732).
[5] MS A has Simēon Ibraimovich.
[6] MS A does not state that he was an Armenian or from Erzerum.

Simēon, the ambassador, thus stayed in Isfahan for two years until the return of Nāder. Nāder then summoned him once more and asked, "Give me the letter from your Tsar and I shall respond." Simēon answered, "I cannot give you that letter, but I can tell you that my Tsar, learning of what you did with the Shah, has sent me an order which states that you are now in control of Persia. Either present the debtor (i.e., the Shah), who resides in Persia, to me, so that I can ask for the money, or give me the sum which he owes us yourself." Nāder answered, "The person who owes you money, owes me as well. He was a madman, who was preoccupied with wine and who foolishly surrendered our country to the Ottomans. As to the debt to your Tsar, I have the following statement: Our Shah did not make war on you, why did you make war on our cities and spend great sums for their conquest? Was anyone threatening Gīlān so that you had to come and defend it for our sake? On what pretense did you take it and keep it for so many years?" This was Nāder's stern response to the envoy. Eleven days later, another envoy, a plenipotentiary ambassador from Moscovy, with a large retinue consisting of 500 men, arrived in Isfahan with great splendor.[1] He was a great nobleman and might have been related to the Tsar of Moscovy.[2] He was met with great honor on his arrival in Isfahan and Nāder ordered that he be provided with all the necessary comforts and foodstuff, including the best wines from [New] Julfa. Six days later the ambassador met Nāder and presented his Tsar's letter. The two conferred and Nader learned of the Tsar's intentions. Returning to his quarters, the ambassador dispatched gifts, consisting of a superb mirror and a very expensive golden clock. Nāder received them and was very pleased.

As we stated previously, however, Nāder had prepared an army to march on Shirvan and Shemakhi and fight the Caucasian Albanians,[3] when he was recalled to fight the Afghans in Herāt. He took the two ambassadors with him and went to Tabriz to prepare his

---

[1]Abraham has *māl*, signifying property.

[2]Prince Sergei Dmitrievich Golitsyn. By this time the tsar was actually Tsarina Anna (1730-1740).

[3]Abraham has *Aghvan*. Not to be confused with *Avghan* (Afghans).

attack. After their arrival there, a new envoy arrived from Moscovy, who relayed the following angry message to Nāder from the Tsar: "Why have you detained two of my ambassadors and are not permitting their departure with your response to my messages?" Nāder then let Simēon go but kept the others for several days. He then released the last ambassador and told him to take the following message to the Tsar: "We are not required to give to you what you ask. If you wish to make war on us we are ready. This is our land. We shall not give you any money." The envoy departed.[1]

Prior to his attack on Shirvan, Nāder marched with his army to the plain of Erevan and pitched his camp there. Erevan was at that time in Ottoman hands. The Ottomans, who had learned of his arrival, did not venture out of the city but remained in the fortress. Nāder then laid siege to Erevan.

The Ottomans did not respond in any way. They did not even fire their cannons once. Instead, they asked for peace terms and said that they were prepared to surrender the city. Nāder ordered that those Ottomans who wished to stay in the city could stay and those who wished to leave could leave freely to wherever they wished. Thus was Erevan taken.[2]The wealthy Muslim notables of Erevan, some four hundred of them, had to pay fifty, forty, twenty, or ten *toman*s each, depending on their status. The Armenians of Erevan were subjected to the same treatment. One of them, the son of Hovakim, was forced to give thirty purses.[3]

---

[1]Golitsyn stayed with Nāder and was responsible for the negotiations, which resulted in the Treaty of Ganǰe (1735).

[2]The chronology is not correct. Erevan surrendered on 3 October 1735, after the capitulation of Ganǰe and Tiflis (July 1735). Nāder's siege of Kars forced the Turks to come to terms and to return to the pre-1723 borders. For more details, see Bournoutian, *The Chronicle of Abraham of Crete*, Chapters XVI-XX. Abraham must have left Erevan after its fall to the Turks in 1724, for his account is brief and inaccurate.

[3]This sentence does not appear in MS B.

XX

How Nāder Took Ganǰe and Shemakhi and How He Attacked the Lesghians. How He Proceeded to Take Georgia and Returned to Erevan

After that, Nāder left part of his army to guard Erevan, while he moved on Ganǰe. He arrived in a settlement called Görük in the local dialect, which is close to Aramuz. Aramuz is on one side of it, Arakhuz on the other, and Aghadzor on the third side. The place was known as Gök-Kilisa. The reason for this name is that there is a blue-colored church there, which, according to ancient tradition, was inhabited by numerous hermits, who, during the reign of Shah 'Abbās, spent their life praying there. Local lore has it that when Shah 'Abbās marched in that direction, water sprang from under the earth and a blue lake appeared in front of him and he could not continue to move forward and reach the village. The Blue Church is located on an island surrounded by the lake on all sides.[1] Shah 'Abbās had invaded the area, for he thought that the inhabitants of that region belonged to an unknown tribe who refused to submit to him. After this providential sign, however, the Shah halted and said, "I shall look into this and find out what contrivance is this?" He sent his men around the region and they brought forth a number of Christians. The Shah asked them, "Who are those people who live in that settlement, where I witnessed such wonders?" Which tribe do they belong to?" They answered, "They are Christian monks who day and night pray to God." The Shah replied, "If they are engaged in prayer, I have nothing against them." From that day forward the place was called Gök-Kilisa, a title given to it by Shah 'Abbās. The place called Arakhuz got its name from the words *khuzum vochkharats*, that is, "shearing sheep," from the wool of which some made clothes for themselves. Aramuz received its name from *mzel*, that is, "milking sheep." All of the above was told to me by the local inhabitants. Let us resume our narrative.

---

[1]Probably refers to the monastery of Hayravank' and the church of The Holy Virgin in Lake Sevan (Gökcha), which in the 18th century was an island in Lake Sevan.

Nāder's army let its horses pasture on the green plain of Görük and stayed there for twenty-five days. It then moved on to the city of Ganǰe, which at that time was in the hands of the Ottomans and full of Turks. The Ottomans met the Persians and a fierce battle ensued for thirty-three days. Blood flooded the field. Nāder defeated the Ottomans and took Ganǰe. Near the city was a village called Kilisa Kend, and many of the Ottomans who fled the battlefield took refuge with the Armenians living there. When Nāder's soldiers learned of this, they went there and slaughtered them all.

Leaving Ganǰe, Nāder advanced to Shemakhi and took it as well as Shirvan. After that, he marched on the Lesghian Tatars, whose leader was called Hāǰǰī Dāvūd Bek. After defeating him, he forced them to pay tribute and took a great deal of money from the land of the Lesghians. He then moved on Tiflis and Georgia, where lofty princes and nobles greeted him and escorted him with great ceremony to Tiflis. Nāder gave them *k̲al'ats*. Since the nobles of Kakhet'i had not appeared, Nāder summoned them as well. They came and greeted him. He presented them with even finer robes and superb horses, for they had not been under the suzerainty of Persia and did not fear Nāder.

After the exchange of pleasantries, Nāder spoke to the leader of the nobles, who was called Zohrab Khan, and asked for his daughter in marriage. Zohrab responded, "I accept and I shall gladly give you my daughter, provided you appoint me the sole ruler[1] of my region." Nāder agreed and declared him the ruler of the Kakhet'i. Suspecting that Zohrab might flee in the night and not give his daughter in marriage, since he, like all the Georgians, was Christian, Nāder assigned men to watch him and to prevent him from escaping. Six days later, Nāder called Zohrab and said, "I asked you to do something and you agreed, what have you done about it?" Zohrab replied, "May God protect you, I have to go and bring my daughter here myself." Nāder answered, "Send a letter to your home ordering her to appear." Zohrab answered, "I shall do as you command." Zohrab then wrote a letter home asking his wife

---

[1]In this case, the *vālī* or regent.

and daughter to come to Tiflis. He explained Nāder's desire to marry the daughter. However, he secretly wrote another note that stated, "Let my subjects know that my so called son-in-law has seized me and has forced me to give my daughter in marriage to him. Do not send my daughter here to marry this heathen."

When his nobles read the second letter, they were filled with rage and prepared to do battle with the unbeliever. They were ready to sacrifice their lives rather than to obey. The messengers thus returned empty-handed. They appeared before Nāder and stated, "The inhabitants of that land did not give us the maiden. They wanted to kill us and we barely escaped with our lives." Nāder then became enraged and told Zohrab, "What have you done? Why didn't you instruct them to send your daughter? They have refused and I shall put you to death." Zohrab replied, "I have no power over my subjects. I have asked them to send my daughter and they have refused. That is why I asked you, my master, to dispatch me as the supreme ruler of my land so that by your order everyone would obey me and I could then order them to carry out your command. But you refused to do so. What can I do now?" Nāder there and then appointed Zohrab the sole ruler, gave him an official decree to that effect, and sent him back to Kakhet'i to force its submission.

Zohrab took the decree affixed with the seal of Nāder and together with two notables of the Khan went to his country. Upon his arrival, the nobles gathered around him and read the decree that appointed Zohrab to govern over them. After conferring, the nobles killed one of the Persian notables who had arrived with Zohrab. They sent the other notable back to Nāder to tell him what had transpired and to declare that they would have no one lording over them. The surviving notable arrived and recounted everything to Nāder, stating, "Zohrab, whom you have appointed as ruler, rose against you and ordered the death of my friend." Nāder was so enraged that he immediately marched against them, but he could not avenge himself. He was defeated, fled back to Tiflis, and did not resume hostilities against them. Since the Ottomans had lost Tiflis,[1] Nāder left Georgia and returned to Erevan. Let us now return to Sultan Mahmut.

XXI

How Nāder Fought a Great Battle Against the Ottomans, Captured Their Commander, 'Abdullah Pasha, and Killed Him. How He Advanced to Hasan Kale and Reached Van. How Nāder was Elected the Shah of the Persians

The Ottomans, as noted, had judged their Sultan, Ahmet, had removed him from the throne, and had installed Sultan Mahmut in his place. The new Sultan appointed Köprülü Ogli 'Abdullah Pasha as the commander-in-chief of the army, and dispatched him to Kars with an army of 300,000 men. Nāder was informed that the Ottomans were advancing towards Persia and he prepared for war. His 75,000-man army consisted of 53,000 cavalry and 12,000 infantry and they were camped between Erevan and Ējmiatsin. After completing his preparations, Nāder marched against the Ottomans in the direction of Tālesh.[2] He arrived in a place called Maghara,[3] close to the Arpa Çay, which is three-days' distance from Tālesh. Nāder had some 28,000 well-equipped horses in reserve. The reason for this was that he planned to cover a three to five days' march in twenty-four hours. He planned to catch the enemy offguard and unprepared for battle and to defeat them in the ensuing panic. During such a forced march many horses would fall and he therefore needed fresh horses to replace them. He left Maghara, crossed the Arpa Çay, and camped at a place called Su-Battan, where he rested.

The Ottomans, hearing of Nāder's advance, built fortified towers[4] and ditches prepared for battle. They stayed behind their fortifications and did not advance toward the Persians. Nāder gathered

---

[1] That is, they had left eastern Georgia for good.
[2] A settlement in the Karbi-Basar *mahal* ("district").
[3] *Mağāra* means "cavern," "grotto," or "ditch."
[4] Abraham uses the Turkish term of *çarkifelek,* which resembles a catapult.

his commanders and said, "Listen, my brave men. If the Ottomans leave their fortifications, God will grant us victory. If they do not venture out, then God shall favor them with victory. We will, therefore, attack now and the minute they shower us with bullets we shall retreat, feigning flight. The moment they come out from behind their fortifications, we shall turn and catch them off guard, attack them and they shall flee in disorder." He then proceeded to attack the Ottomans.

At their first encounter, Nāder retreated. The Persians fell back for an hour, creating the illusion that they were fleeing the battlefield. When the Ottomans witnessed the feigned flight, they abandoned their barriers and sped after the Persian army. The Ottoman army was so large that the human eye, even from above, could not fit it in a single frame. All the ravines, rocks, cliffs, mountains, hills, and plains were filled with Ottoman soldiers, which resembled worms crawling on the surface of the earth. When the retreat was sufficient enough to lure all the Ottomans out of their bastions, Nāder turned his army to face the enemy. The two armies clashed and began to slaughter each other. God have mercy! The entire plain was filled with corpses and the soil was covered with the blood of fighting men. Stones, shrubs, and earth were no longer visible, rather only bodies of the fallen men and dead horses were visible. One could not pass without stepping over the dead. Nāder was victorious over the Ottoman army. He beat them back to Manzikert and Hasan Kale. 'Abdullah Pasha was caught and brought to Nāder, who killed him.[1] He buried him and erected a roofed mausoleum over his grave, so that it would proclaim Nāder's victory over the Turks.[2] The Persians took much loot from the Ottoman army.

Nāder then advanced with his army to the outskirts of Van. Here he evacuated all the villages, which were populated by Armenian subjects of the Ottomans. He took tens of thousands of young men, women and children captive and sent them to Ḵorāsān.

---

[1] The actual account differs. He was killed in the battle of Eghvard on 19 June 1735, see Bournoutian, *The Chronicle of Abraham of Crete*, pp. 39-40.

[2] Such a monument was indeed constructed, *Ibid.*, pp. 42-44.

He then went back to Persia, but did not go to Isfahan. Rather, he camped in a place called the Moğān.[1] He sent messengers to the various notables of Persia to appear before him. He invited them to a national assembly, conferred with them, and stated the following, "Do you know why I have summoned you? It has been many years that I have taken up the sword in your name, have fought the enemy, and have driven the Afghans, Ottomans, and Moscovites out of our Persian cities. Having accomplished that, I have now come here so that you will elect a new Shah." The notables heard his speech and remained silent. He repeated his words three times. Then two of the great nobles answered thus: "Lord, since you mentioned it in your speech, with your approval we would like you to bring Shah Ṭahmāsp back to the throne to rule over us." Angered by their response, Nāder ordered their execution and they were killed. He then repeated his speech and asked, "What is your decision?" Filled with terror, they thrice uttered in unison, "You are our Shah." Nāder then answered, "If you truly wish me to accept[2] the throne, you have to give me your mandate in writing." They all wrote their names and affixed their seals to the document attesting that "Nāder is our Shah and we recognize no other sovereign." They presented him with the document of investiture, prepared a celebration that lasted many days and made him Shah.[3] After that, Nāder dispatched an envoy, 'Abdullah Pasha,[4] to the Ottoman Sultan Mahmut, asking him to return every[5] Persian prisoner of war. The Sultan received the ambassador with great honor and ordered that they gather Persian prisoners from every province, set them free, and let them go back to their homeland. This was carried out as thoroughly as was possible. Thus Nāder became the

---

[1]Text erroneously has *Damoghan* (Dāmğān), which is in Persian `Araq.

[2]Text has the Persian term *qabūl* (signifying agreement or acceptance).

[3]Although briefly stated, this account of Nāder's elevation to the throne does not differ from all other primary sources.

[4]The envoy was not a pasha, but a Persian notable called 'Abdul Qolī Khan Zangane. A Turkish Pasha, Ganǰ 'Alī, the former governor of Ganǰe, accompanied the Persian envoy.

[5]Text has the Persian term *har qadar*.

Shah of the Persians and a peace treaty was concluded between the Persians and Ottomans.[1]

The End
Amen[2]

Chapter XXII[3]
[*Nāder's Campaigns, 1736-1738*]

Nāder stayed on the Moğān for forty days to receive the customary official congratulations and the offerings from the various Persian notables. His treasury was filled with cash and precious stones. The Ottoman Sultan's envoy arrived with a letter which stated, "Release your Shah, restore him to the throne, and we shall conclude a peace with you." Nāder answered, "When you put your legal Sultan back on the throne, I shall follow suit." The Turks, as noted, had deposed Sultan Ahmet and had put Sultan Mahmut in his place. The Sultan responded, "Sultan Ahmet was not a fortunate[4] man. We removed him and replaced him with another." Nāder replied, "Just like your Sultan, my Shah was not a fortunate man either. I have therefore replaced him and have taken his crown." Realizing their hopeless situation, the Ottomans concluded peace.

Nāder Shah[5] then left the Moğān and went against the Lesghians. He reached a village called Ērkach', located in the highlands. There is a large mount called Kara Murad by the Muslims and Tsaghkēvanots' by the Armenians. He had to pass this mountain to

---

[1]This sentence is absent from MS A.

[2]MS B has nine additional folios [83a-87a], which is a partial list of the various cities, rivers, and other geographical locations in the text.

[3]MS A has twelve additional folios, which are larger and written on a different paper. The first two folios [87a-87b] repeat the details of Nader's election. Folios 88a-90b are the continuation of the narrative up to the conquest of Qandahār and the restoration the borders of the Ṣafavid State. The rest are blank. The heading does not appear in MSS A or B, but was added by the translator.

[4]Abraham has the western term *fortuna.*

[5]Abraham now refers to Nader as *kaysar* ("Ceasar"), hereinafter Shah.

reach the Lesghians. One early morning he saw that this mount and its valleys were inundated with snakes. He could not cross it. Nāder Shah was amazed. He summoned his reputable astronomers and philosophers and asked them, "How is it that my path is filled with so many snakes?" They replied, "Once every thirty years, the snakes have a battle on Mount Masis,[1] where the king of the serpents is located. This is the aftermath of that encounter. Nāder Shah then ordered that some 600 to 700 men from the village of Shankvan, a settlement of some 2000 to 3000 households, be brought over. They were expert snake catchers and snake charmers, who were called *sunjis*.[2] They managed to catch and kill all the snakes. They then covered them with gunpowder[3] and burned them.[4] The troops then passed without further delay and entered Lesghian territory. They fought and defeated the Lesghians and Nāder Shah took over their land.

Nāder Shah then returned to Persia and marched on Qandahār with 180,000 well-armed and well-equipped men. Eighty days later, he reached the outskirts of the city and camped some six-hours' distance from it. He sent a messenger asking the Afghans to surrender the fortress. They responded, "We shall not surrender." Nāder Shah became angry and ordered 'Alī Qolī Khan of K̲orāsān to raid and kill the inhabitants of the surrounding villages, which he did for twenty-eight days. In addition, Nāder managed to block the road from Kabul and did not permit Afghan reinforcements to reach Qandahār. There were 134,000 Afghans in Qandahār, however, hence they had enough troops to resist the Persians.

Nāder Shah totally surrounded Qandahār and laid siege to it for nine months.[5] After nine months he approached the city and came close to its high walls. Qandahār is a fine city; few can match its beauty and prosperity. It is located on such a high ground that one

---

[1] Another name for Mt. Ararat.

[2] Probably named after the Sunja range and river in Daghestan.

[3] The text has the Persian term *bārūt*.

[4] This curious episode is not mentioned in any other source.

[5] In order to withstand the winter, Nāder built a completely new city two miles southeast of Qandahār, called Nāderābād.

feels close to the stars.[1] Nāder Shah was determined to take it. After a long delay, he finally decided to act. He unsheathed his sword and advanced at the head of his troops. His troops followed the Shah, not fearing the blades or the fire of the enemy. The Afghans threw large stones from the fortress on the heads of the Persians. They fell from such a height that they shattered into a thousand pieces. God Have Mercy! The earth and sky shook. The Persians finally entered the city. After nine days of fierce and bloody fighting, the Afghans were put to the sword. Nāder Shah took Qandahār.[2]

The End
Amen

---

[1]The fort was built by the Qaitul Ridge. It had enormous walls, some of them 30 feet thick.

[2]The fort was raised and the inhabitants were moved to Nāderābād.

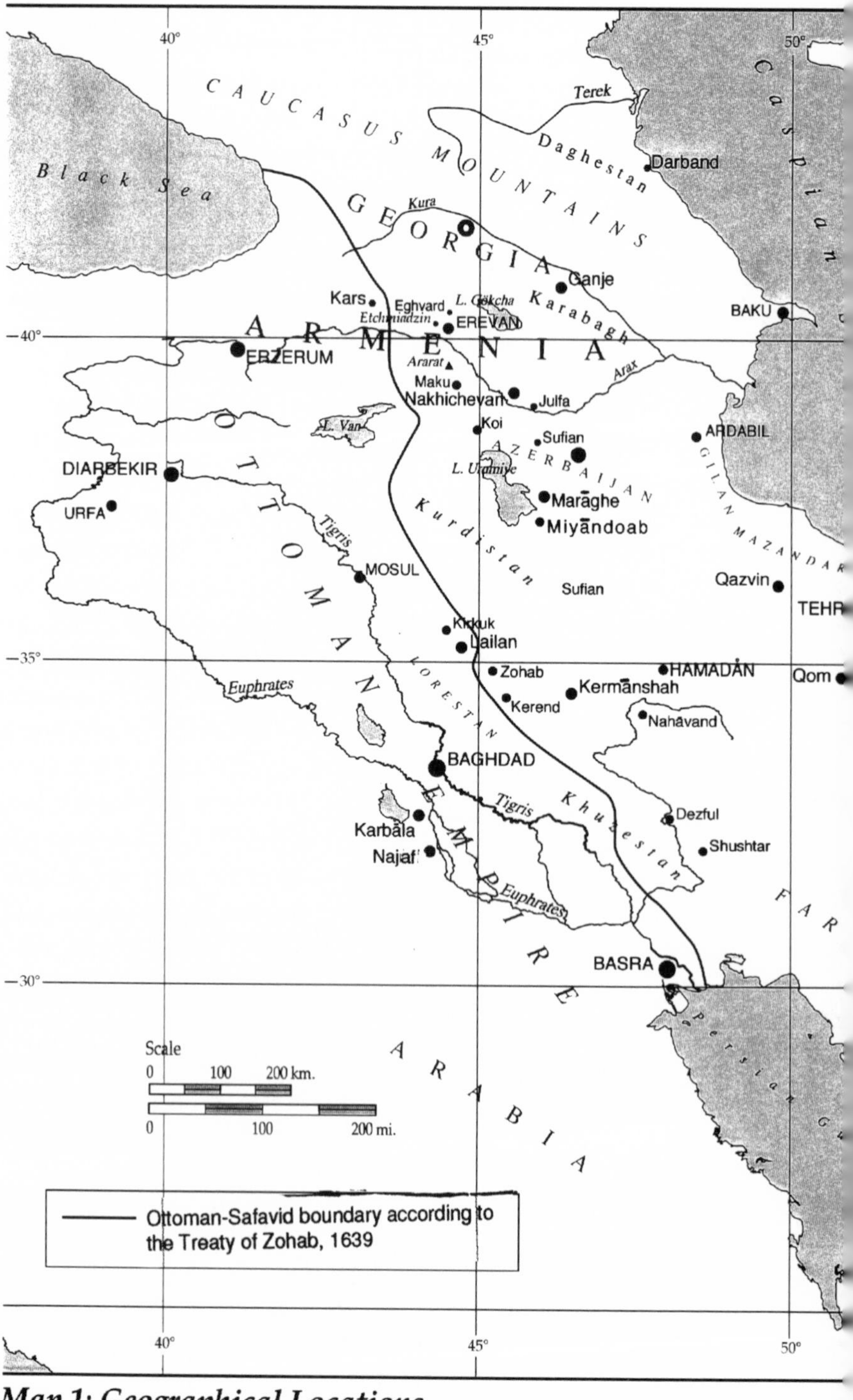

Map 1: Geographical Locations

55°
60°
TRANSOXIANA
KHWARAZM
40°
TURKISTAN
Atrak R.
KORĀSĀN
Astarabad
MAŠHAD
ZANDARAN
QOHESTĀN
35°
HERĀT
AFGHANISTAN
SFAHAN
r Jugha (New Julfa)
KERMĀN
QANDAHĀR
Kermān
30°
SHIRAZ
Lar
BANDAR 'ABBAS
BALUCHISTAN
55°
60°
Robert H. Hewsen

ntioned in the Text

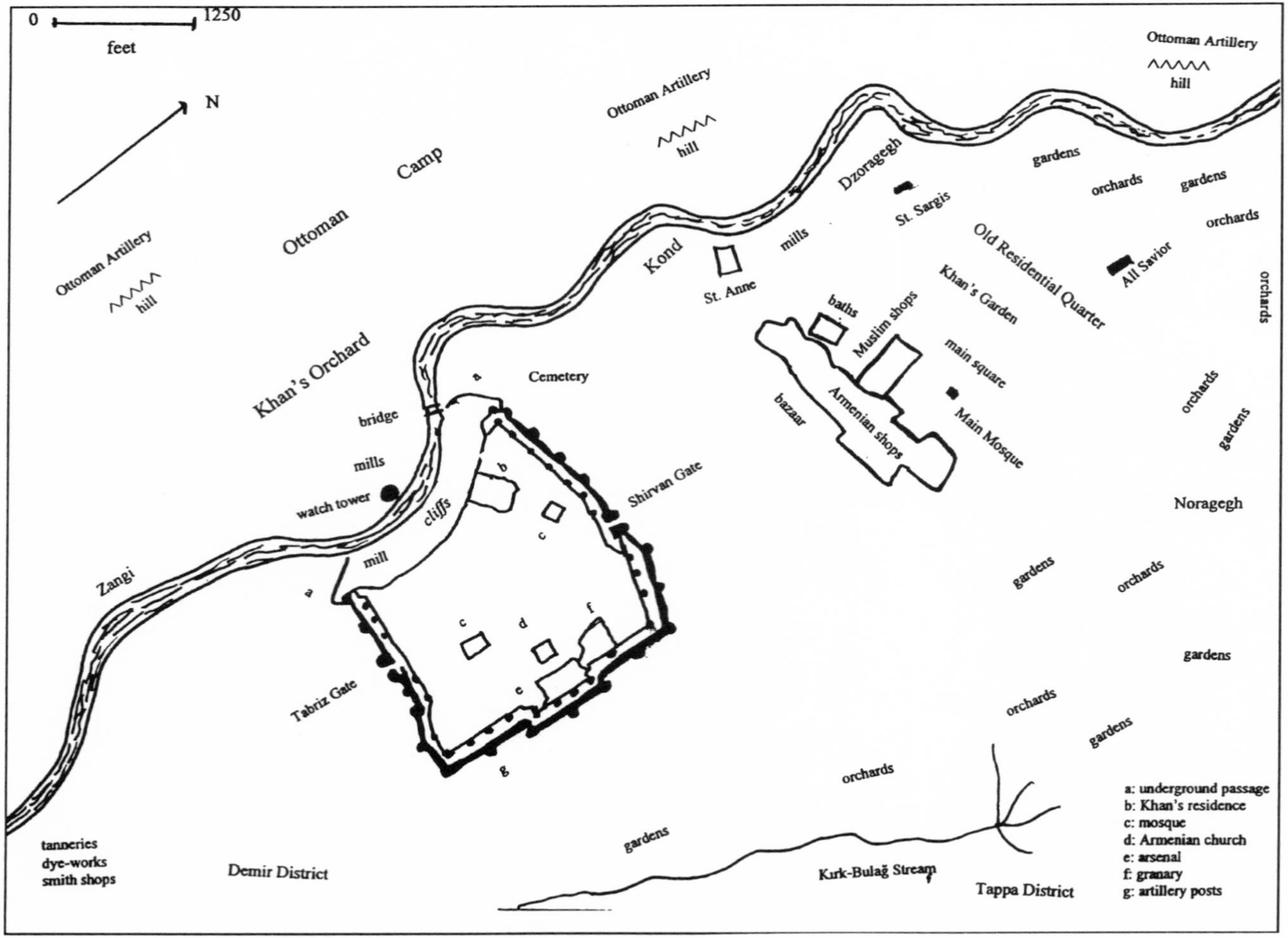
0
1250
feet
N
Ottoman Artillery
hill
Ottoman Camp
Ottoman Artillery
hill
Ottoman Artillery
hill
Khan's Orchard
bridge
mills
watch tower
cliffs
mill
Zangi
Cemetery
Kond
St. Anne
mills
Dzoragegh
St. Sargis
Old Residential Quarter
Khan's Garden
All Savior
gardens
orchards
gardens
orchards
orchards
baths
Muslim shops
main square
Main Mosque
bazaar
Armenian shops
Shirvan Gate
Tabriz Gate
Noragegh
gardens
orchards
gardens
orchards
gardens
gardens
orchards
orchards
gardens
Kırk-Bulağ Stream
Tappa District
Demir District
tanneries
dye-works
smith shops
a: underground passage
b: Khan's residence
c: mosque
d: Armenian church
e: arsenal
f: granary
g: artillery posts

Map 2. The City and Fortress of Erevan during the Siege of 1724.

The battle between Nāder and the Ottoman general, Topal Osman Pasha, outside Baghdad (1733). A group of Nāder's men, entrenched on the mountainside, open fire on the Ottomans.

Source: *J̌ahāngošāy-e Nāderī*, illustration No 6.

The battle of Eghvard (1735) between Nāder and the Ottoman general, ʿAbdullah Pasha. The Persian army has routed the Ottomans. The corps of ʿAbdulah Pasha is on the ground under the foot of Nāder's horse.

Source: *Jahāngošāy-e Nāderī*, illustration No 7.

Select Bibliography

Abraham Erewants'i. *Patmut'iwn paterazmats'n, 1721-1736 t'owi.* Venice [San Lazzaro], 1977.

_____. *Patmut'iwn paterazmats'n, 1721-1736.* Yerevan, 1938.

_____. *Istoriia voin, 1721-1736. Erevan*, 1939.

_____. *Omebis istoria.* Tbilisi, 1976.

Adamec, Ludwig, ed. *Historical Gazetteer of Iran.* Graz, 1976-1989.

Arunova, M. R. and Ashrafian, K. Z. *Gosudarstvo Nadir-Shakha Afshara.* Moscow, 1958.

Barsamian, Kh. *The Calendar of the Armenian Church.* New York, 1995.

Birashk, A. *A Comparative Calendar of the Iranian, Muslim Lunar, and Christian Eras.* New York, 1992.

Bournoutian, G. A. *The Khanate of Erevan under Qajar Rule, 1795-1828.* Costa Mesa, 1992.

_____. *A History of Qarabagh.* Costa Mesa, 1994.

_____. *Russia and the Armenians of Transcaucasia: A Documentary Record, 1797-1889.* Costa Mesa, 1998.

_____. *The Chronicle of Abraham of Crete.* Costa Mesa, 1999.

_____. "The Armenian Community of Isfahan in the Seventeenth century," *The Armenian Review* 24-25 (1971-1972), 27-45, 33-50.

A Chronicle of the Carmelites in Persia and the Papal Mission of the 17th and 18th centuries. London, 1939.

Fraser, J. *The History of Nadir Shah.* London, 1742.

Gilanentz, Petros Di Sarkis. *The Chronicle of Petros Di Sarkis Di Gilanentz.* Lisbon, 1959.

Hakob Shemakhets'i. *Pokhodi Takhmasp Kuli-Khana i izbranie ego shakhom.* Erevan, 1932.

Hakobyan, T'. Kh. *Erevani patmut'iwnē, 1500-1800*. Erevan, 1971.

Hammer-Purgstall, Baron J. von. *Historire de l'Empire Ottoman*. Vol. IV, Tehran (Persian translation), 1368/1989.

Hanway, J. *An Historical Account of the British Trade over the Caspian Sea*. London, 1753.

Krusinski, J. D. *The History of the Late Revolutions of Persia*. London, 1740.

Lang, D. M. *The Last Years of the Georgian Monarchy, 1658-1832*. New York, 1967.

Lockhart, L. *Nadir Shah*. London, 1938.

_____. *The Fall of the Safavi Dynasty and the Afghan Occupation of Persia*. Cambridge, 1958.

Maksoudian. Krikor. *Chosen of God: The Election of the Catholicos of All Armenians*. New York, 1995.

Moḥammad Mahdī Kowkabī Astarābādī, Mīrzā. *J̌ahāngošāy-e Nāderī*. Tehran, 1341/1962.

Moḥammad Kāżem Marvī. *'Ālam-ārāy-e Nāderī*. Tehran, 1368/1990.

Qodūsī, Moḥammad Ḥosein. *Nāder-nāme*. Mašhad, 1339/1960.

Index

Transcaucasia, 1-3, 7, 17
Tsaghkevanots‘, 95
Turkmen, 65

Ulugerd, 58
Urfa, 57. *See also* Edessa.
Urumiye (lake), 36
Üsküdar, 50
Uzbeks, 63-64

Van, 92-93
Venice, 4

Wakhtang VI (Georgian king), 14-17
Wakhusht (Georgian prince), 16

Yalğuz Ḥasan, 8, 18
Yangiǰe, 42
Yazd, 55

Zafran (stream), 47
Zafran (village), 49
Zaghu (Zağe), 40
Zagros (mountains), 73
Zahtarān (fort), 55, 58-59
Zamburak, 50
Zangane (Kurdish tribe), 39
Zangane (river), 75
Zangi (river), 23, 26-29, 34
Zāyandeh (river), 70
Zelal, 37-39
Zohāb (Zuhab), 40, 47, 49, 66, 66, 74-75, 77, 80-81
Zohāb (treaty of), 1
Zohrab Khan, 90-91

About the Author

George Bournoutian is Professor of East European and Middle Eastern History at Iona College. He has taught Iranian history at UCLA and Armenian history at Columbia University, New York University, Rutgers University, Tufts University, University of Connecticut, and Ramapo College. In addition to seven previous volumes on Armenian, Russian and Iranian history, he is the author of chapters in books edited by Professors Hovannisian, Suny, Chaqueri, and Castriota, as well as a frequent contributor to scholarly journals and encyclopedias.

About the Illustrations

The cover illustration shows Nāder's battle against the Afghans near Mūrčeḵort, Isfahan (November, 1729), from a 1757 illustrated manuscript of *J̌ahāngošāy-e Nāderī* by Mīrzā Moḥammad Mahdī Astarābādī in the private collection of Mr. Abdolali Adib Barumand. The illustration, measuring 17x20 cm., depicts the Afghans fleeing before Nāder's army. He is seen on horseback on the battlefield. Three persons are standing in front of him, two of them being Naṣrollah Mīrzā and Mīrzā Mahdī. Four other illustrations from the same source are reproduced inside this volume (pp. vi, viii, 101, 102).